Good Form

Equestrian Etiquette

Compass Points for Riders

Good Form
Equestrian Etiquette

Toni Cadden

COMPASS
EQUESTRIAN

Henley-in-Arden

Edited by Martin Diggle
Editorial Assistant Clare Harris
Design Alan Hamp
Illustrated by Maggie Raynor

British Library Cataloguing in Publication Data
A catalogue record for this book is available from the British Library

ISBN 1-900667-23-1

Published in Great Britain in 2002 by
Compass Equestrian Limited
Cadborough Farm,
Oldberrow, Henley-in-Arden
Warwickshire, B95 5NX

Printed in Great Britain
by Ebenezer Baylis, Worcester

Contents

Preface *9*

Introduction *11*

1 **Riding out** *15*
on the road *15*
in the country *19*
rights of way *25*
by the sea *22*
jumping on the beach *22*
riding with others *23*
jumping in company *23*
courtesy check list *24*

2 **Buying and Selling** *25*
golden rules of buying *29*
courtesy check list *31*
selling *32*
courtesy check list *34*

3 **Does size matter ?** *36*
courtesy check list *38*

4   **Keeping a Horse at Livery**   *39*
    communication   *41*
    consideration   *43*
    courtesy check list   *44*
    the yard owner's viewpoint *45*
    courtesy check list   *47*

5   **Cherish your Farrier**   *49*
    think ahead   *50*
    courtesy check list   *51*

6   **Dressage – Equestrian Ballet**   *53*
    courtesy check list   *55*

7   **Leaping Ahead – Cross Country Riding**   *57*
    pleasure rides   *57*
    horse trials and hunter trials   *58*
    drag hunting   *61*
    courtesy list (competitive cross country riding)   *63*
    courtesy list (non-competitive cross country riding)   *63*

8   **Over the Top – Show Jumping**   *65*
    courtesy check list   *66*

9   **Show Business**   *69*
    Some basic pointers   *70*
    side-saddle   *71*
    help from the ground   *71*

at the showground 72
in the ring 73
judging 77
courtesy check list 78

10 **A Word about Ponies and Pony Club** 80
Pony Club parents 81
Pony Club instructors 82
ponies 83
courtesy check list 84

11 **In the Driving Seat** 85
requirements for driving 86
basic principles 87
courtesy check list - general driving 89
competing 91
courtesy check list novice whips at shows 93
advice from experts 93
harness racing 95
courtesy check list - harness racing 96

12 **Mapping it out – Long Distance and Endurance Riding** 98
on the ride 101
courtesy check list 102

13 **On Saying Goodbye** 104
care in the twighlight years 104
your final choice 105
courtesy check list - the final courtesy 107

Preface

'With one foot already in the stirrup'
Cervantes (1547-1616)

Educated at a convent high school I was brought up to regard manners as an integral part of daily living and I have been saddened by the decline of courtesy over the years. It doesn't cost anything to be polite and it oils the wheels of daily living in an increasingly whirlwind culture of snap decisions and frenzied activity.

In an equestrian context, there are many verbal maxims and gems of knowledge which used to be passed on from generation to generation. Many of these by design or extension gave instruction on etiquette. However, since the end of the Second World War, there have been on-going changes in the social climate. There is no longer the large number of families owning horses, nor men and women working with them and the chain of information has been broken. People with no previous experience of equines coming to love and own horses are thrown into an abyss sometimes floundering in a sea of well-meaning, but conflicting advice.

This book has been written in an attempt to address this loss of valuable information and I sincerely hope it will be helpful. In an attempt to retain clarity throughout, I have called the horse 'he' and the rider 'she' and trust my readers to adapt this to their own particular circumstances. Please note that the book is not intended to be a book of rules. Readers who are interested in a particular competitive discipline should study and abide by the relevant rule book.

Horses need educating

Introduction

Manners maketh man
William of Wykeham (1324-1404)

Etiquette could be assumed to be old-fashioned and out of date in the hectic climate of fast communication, ideas and action today.

But nowhere has it retained its importance more than in the world of the horse. There are usually right and wrong methods of doing everything and if you only know the right rules and acceptable practice you are halfway towards achieving your goal, whatever that may be.

Manners maketh man, so the adage goes; and that applies to women, horses, dogs etc. Etiquette or good form is not just about saying 'thank you' for a birthday or Christmas present, hospitality or a kindness performed. Much more is involved. It should permeate the whole of life in our attitude towards those with whom we come into contact, both human and animal. It is, after all, only the common courtesy one affords to another. It is a two-way transaction.

While you treat your horse in the best way you know, he must return the compliment, in the stable and out of it. Some behaviour is unacceptable on both sides.

You would not dream of giving him his meal before his water, nor exercising him immediately after a meal. Equally, he knows not to push or barge you about in the stable, and that squashing you against the wall, or kicking, do not enter the equation! You always give yourself sufficient time to tack him up before exercising and he knows that he stands quietly while this is done. He will drop his head for bridling and stand quietly and still to be mounted.

When you open the stable door to lead him out, he walks calmly forward without rushing. When being turned out in the field he waits obediently while you walk him round to face the entrance and shut the gate before releasing him. 'If only!' I hear you say, but none of these things happen automatically, unfortunately. It is all learned behaviour on the part of the horse and kind and patient training on your side.

His good behaviour must extend towards all those who have dealings with him, indeed, everybody. People who say, 'My horse will not let anybody catch/ride him except me' are not doing themselves, or their horse any favours. This is all well and good when you are fit and at home. However, most of us become ill occasionally and it is a real pain for a stand-in groom to deal with a horse who is constantly pushing past and looking over the stable door for someone who is not there.

Also, events do occur when an 'away visit' without a horse is necessary. Such realities should be considered before spoiling an equine. Horses and ponies should be treated like children, with love, kindness, discipline and education. That way you will have a friend to be proud of at home and elsewhere. The combination of affection and obedience make a horse/dog a pleasant companion and the sight of a thoughtful rider who cares about her willing mount's well being is a pleasure. Horses must be well behaved in the stable, paddocks, in hand, ridden and when travelling.

Your horse must behave when the farrier visits. The job will be completed more quickly and efficiently on a horse who stands patiently than one who fidgets and is restless. All these things should have been taught to a young horse before backing, but many of us have bought 'made' horses whose manners left much to be desired.

A horse who will stand square when asked is a real joy to ride and own. Very slowly count the words, 'One Mississippi', 'Two 'Mississippi' Three Mississippi' 'Four Mississippi', and then walk forwards. (This is a first step towards dressage training and an invaluable lesson learned for hacking on the road). It goes without saying that a horse must stand absolutely still while being mounted. A horse should never start to move away before being asked and, finally, a horse who behaves equally well alone and in company is a pleasure to know.

Obviously you do not mount your horse, yelling and kicking to go and yanking the reins to stop while barging past, and into, others at the same time. But some are in such a rush to get on with the riding that the stable management side of things can be neglected.

Handle your horse often in the stable. Tie him up and teach him to move away from you when necessary. Be sure he moves away from the door when you wish to go in and will have his feet picked out, his head, legs (especially hind) and stomach groomed without fuss. It is a good idea to have dogs living around horses. Sometimes, usually when young, they will chase them round the field and, in the end, the horses do not bother, which means that, when chased while being ridden out, they will not take off because they are used to the situation. (Obviously, dogs who snap at the legs of horses and attempt to bite must be corrected).

Good manners on the part of the rider and obedience and a willingness to do whatever is asked of him on the side of the horse are prerequisites for a successful working relationship. Probably the greatest courtesy you could ever pay your young horse would be to have him trained by the Monty Roberts 'join up' method of schooling. 'Breaking in' is such a damning expression. We do not want our horses broken in spirit or body. We want them to be healthy, obedient and happy to work with us. Be sure the trainer is one of Monty's accredited trainers and watch the demonstrations whenever you can. HRH Queen Elizabeth II was so impressed by him that she invited him to spend a week at Windsor Castle as her guest where he demonstrated 'join up' with his advance and retreat methods. Monty believes horses should be doing things because they want to, not because we want them to and what could be fairer than that?

Only if you are riding for the right reasons will you really enjoy it and employ good manners, thoughtfulness and kindness towards other people and their horses. It will not work if you are riding because your neighbour owns a horse, or you live in the country and it seems the right thing to do, or by riding you hope you will meet the 'right people', whoever they may be, or you have time on your hands and are bored with watching Western films on television.

Riding requires hard work, dedication, a great deal of time and an endless love of the horse.

Riding Out

The hoof with a galloping sound is
shaking the powdery plain.
Aeneid (bk. 8, 1.596)

There can be do doubt that riding is addictive. The more you ride, the more you want to and the more enjoyable it becomes. Perhaps the greatest joy of equestrianism is riding out, or hacking. To be alone, or in company, with a well-mannered horse in the countryside on a beautiful day must rank as one of the greatest of life's pleasures.

We horsemen and women all have our memories, but my most vivid recollection is being with a group cantering round the edge of Lake Windermere early one morning. It was late spring and there was the usual Lake District mist like a fine veil covering the water. Bluebells, primroses, snowdrops, aconites and other wild flowers were blooming and there was a hint of sunshine to come. The scene was idyllic and all the riders were enchanted by the occasion. It was as if we wanted to capture the perfect moment and hold it forever. Spellbound by the magic of the pastoral scene, we were all locked into a time warp where nothing else mattered. So much so that not a word was spoken until the lake was far behind. Apart from the birdsong continuing the dawn chorus, the only other sound was the gentle, rhythmic, thudding of hooves on the woodland floor. All though nothing was said, we felt privileged to be part of such a satisfying experience.

On the Road

It is a sad reflection of the times that in many parts of the country bridleways are hard to find and riding tracks few and far between. Most responsible riders will be members of the British Horse Society and it is they who have done the spade work towards getting more bridleways opened up. This means money, and it is membership subscriptions which help to pay for this and other campaigns, such as road safety advertisements, broadcasting the need for reflective clothing at night, the introduction of the Riding and Road Safety Test, and so on.

However, some road work will be inevitable but wherever you ride, there will be rules and regulations to observe. The rider who gallops everywhere without concern for crops, wildlife and other people is a liability and will give other, careful riders a bad reputation.

To ride out in company, of course, your horse needs good manners and if you ride alone he still needs to be obedient and under control at all times. If not, he is a hazard both to you and to other road users. If you think your horse may be nervous, ride with experienced horses as companions. If your horse does play up, don't block the road. Try to get him safely out of the way until he has calmed down.

A horse must be as traffic-proof as possible before venturing out on public roads. We all know that some horses will pass a revving vehicle happily yet shy at a falling leaf. This is why you must be a safe rider with an independent seat so that you can cope with any situation which might arise.

Be alert. Riding a horse is like driving a car in so far as you must be ready for any eventuality. Don't go off into a personal day-dream. You can enjoy your ride whilst still being in charge and aware of what others might do. Always keep your eyes open for man-hole covers on verges and on the road itself. A horse's metal shoe stepping on one can induce a dangerous skid. Avoid them at all costs.

Never ride without saddle and bridle and proper riding clothes with boots and hat. In narrow roads ride single file and never ride more than two abreast. Keep a young horse on the inside and keep both hands on the reins unless signalling direction. Keep both feet in the stirrups and never carry anything which could upset your balance or your horse and certainly not a second rider.

Never assume anything. Ensure that you will be seen by wearing light, bright clothing if it is likely to become dull and, it goes without saying, always wear a hat. You only have one head so it is common-sense to look after it. Reflective clothing and stirrup lights are essential if you must ride at dusk or after dark; but check that your horse's tail is not so long that it obscures your lights from the rear.

I don't believe in the bomb-proof horse. By their very nature equines are unpredictable animals, with rapid flight being their instinctive response to something frightening.

Bin bags by the side of the road, accompanied by terrifying looking rubbish, falling leaves whisking in front of his face, oncoming large vehicles, a tractor or indeed most agricultural machinery, the list is almost endless for producing a genuine fear response or an excuse to be skittish. Someone putting up an umbrella suddenly will make most horses freak out; as will a piece of plastic floating across the road like Casper the ghost. A pony and trap will often cause a similar reaction and a lorry behind you trying to be kind by stopping with a hiss of air brakes never fails to produce chaos!

Cars towing caravans or boats are possibly the most dangerous of all. The car draws alongside and that is all right. When this is followed by the length of the towed object most horses are seriously worried. Too many people who tow caravans are not sufficiently competent at judging distances. They think they are driving their car and forget the wide load following, sometimes with tragic consequences. So it pays to keep your wits about you and have an occasional glance behind to see what is coming so you can plan accordingly.

Cyclists need consideration too. It is a good idea to ride out sometimes with a cyclist and this accustoms the horse to them.

It is easy, but dangerous, to switch off completely with your mind on other things. I was hacking along quite happily one day when a fire engine screeched round the corner switching on the siren as it came. My unfortunate horse exploded and bolted, fortunately forward. So you just never know what is around the bend, literally!

Give clear signals to other road users. They must be clear as to what you are going to do, especially which way you are going. Be sure there is no confusion. Be seen and be safe. Look out for tractors, stray dogs, cyclists, motor cyclists, pneumatic drills, road works, in fact anything unusual which might spook your mount.

Drivers listening to music, or talking on a mobile 'phone or to other passengers, may not have total concentration so it is up to you to take care at all times. (If you take a mobile 'phone with you while out hacking make sure it is switched off before you put one foot in the stirrup, or you might set off faster than you intended!)

Any excuse

Keep your Cool

Always acknowledge a driver's courtesy towards you. Some drivers only have to see a horse ridden on the road to suffer an immediate fit of pique or even actual road rage. If it is any consolation, these people often feel the same about pedestrians and cyclists and probably other car drivers! I have a theory it has something to do with road tax and the fact that some car drivers take the view that they pay to use the roads and we don't. This is an erroneous idea to which riders should not give credence. Road tax is not a toll; it is simply a form of indirect taxation. There is currently no connection between revenue raised through road tax and money spent on building or maintaining roads. Most roads are public highways upon which anyone is permitted to travel, free of charge, provided they observe the relevant laws.

However it is a sad fact that goodwill between horse riders and other traffic is quickly lost, so be sure that you are the polite one. There will always be faults on both sides. I knew a rider hacking out with a friend who was incensed when a car squeezed between her and the other horse. She was so angry that she banged on the roof of the offending car with her whip. Luckily, no one was hurt, but the outcome could have been very different. It is often difficult to know the right way to react to gross bad manners and the moment usually passes so quickly that we don't always react as perhaps we should.

Another rider acquaintance felt that all drivers should submit to allowing her and her horse complete right of way. So confident of her priority over other road users was she that when she dropped her whip, which was quite often, she would signal to a car driver, in front or behind, to slow down, and then wait while they stopped their car, got out and picked up the stick and returned it to her. No wonder some people are anti-horse riders!

In The Country

If riding in the country always wish people a 'good morning' and remember to shut gates after you. If someone opens one and shuts it behind you, remember to thank them. Look out for livestock and don't gallop anywhere near them. If you see stock in trouble, for example a sheep lying on its back or caught in wire or brambles, do find some way of notifying the relevant farmer. If you cannot do it, ask another to do it for you.

In some ways country riding can be as hazardous as being on the road. There is always the possibility of the unexpected, no matter how well you think you know the route. A farmer inspecting his crops may leave his Landrover parked round the corner on the bridleway; a new fence may be erected, a tree may have fallen on to the track or a tractor may be making more noise than usual. One of my most alarming incidents occurred when I rounded a bend to be confronted with the fierce spray from a water sprinkler in the field.

We have all been driving along in our car when we have suddenly spotted a perfect place to ride. The thought is there immediately. 'I will bring my horse here one day.' Of course, this cannot be done without prior permission of the landowner or local authority or whoever it is who has the rights to the land. It could even be dangerous if the land is used for shooting or archery, or it could have been left to grow for suitable grazing in the future.

Woods and certain areas of forestry, moorland and heath may be used by the military and need extra caution. If there is a red flag flying, don't even think about entering the area.

One day, when not concentrating I went into a wood by a side path and both my horse and I were astonished when the bushes along the track got up and walked away. The army is very good at disguise!

Rights of Way

Some farmers are happy to let riders use their fields, perhaps where there is 'set aside', so long as they keep to the headlands and ride round the hedgerows, never across the middle. It is essential to maintain good relationships with local farmers. One who consistently ploughs up his bridleways will need special attention, perhaps an initial telephone call requesting a chat about the situation.

Be sure to park your trailer or horse box where no one will be inconvenienced, not where you will be stuck in the mud when trying to leave and not so that you will have to reverse.

Riders are legally entitled to use bridleways, but do not have exclusive use of them. This distinction is important in terms of etiquette of shared use. Do respect the rights of way you already have. For example, cantering along when it is wet and muddy will cause large ruts from the horse's hooves which, when dried out, could have dangerous consequences for another horse stumbling on the uneven ground when it dries up.

The best solution for those of us who do not have a Dartmoor on our doorstep, is to keep to the official bridleways set up locally. They are on the increase so things should improve.

Riders are not entitled to use footpaths. However, in some places footpaths run alongside a bridleway, so a careful watch has to be kept for walkers and, in some cases, cyclists and others who may have shared right of use.

A rider who was unaware of the concept of ramblers and shared use was cantering along the bridleway when she came to a bend, only to be confronted by a family of walkers striding abreast of the track. Instantly pulling her horse up, he stopped on a sixpence and she flew over the top landing on her feet in front of the walkers. I don't think at that juncture, any of the group thought the combined use was a good idea.

Don't be in the position of having to stop on a sixpence

By the Sea

If you wish to ride on a beach there are rules to obey and it would be sensible to consult the local council by-laws before setting off. Some councils do not allow horses on the beach at all. Others have rules about the times you can ride.

On many beaches, as the tide goes out, there is generally a generous amount of firm, wet beach suitable for riding on. Always walk the going before you gallop. It is hard to tell at speed, when the sand is wet, where the muddy patches are, and where, the day before, children have dug holes and built sandcastles with moats. Never ride below the water line, you might sink in the mud. Never ride along the top where the going is deep sand and, once again, you might sink and also be an inconvenience to other beach users. Riding right along the edge of the sea would be a nuisance to those wanting to paddle, especially children.

Obviously, it should go without saying, you should not consider riding along a beach in the summer when holiday makers are enjoying themselves. You will not be popular if your horse relieves himself on the sand (in some counties you are required to clear up after your horse!) or shies in front of people.

It could also be very dangerous with young children and toddlers who may not see you coming. Of course, if you choose to ride at dawn you might get away with it.

Similarly, if you have the facility of a sea wall there are rules to conform to. A sea wall is, naturally, a defence against the sea encroaching on the land and, while it is okay for walkers to stroll along the top, it is a definite no-go area for horses and their riders. It may be possible to ride along the track, if there is one, below it, though in some areas this land may be owned by the farmer who is adjacent to it, so, again, permission would have to be sought.

Jumping on the Beach

If you are thinking of jumping breakwaters great care must be taken to see that there are no people in the way. Ride along the beach assessing the jumps before you attempt them. Remember that each tide can change the level of the sand or shingle. An even sided jump one day can be a big drop the next. Sand can turn to sinking mud into which landing can strain the horse's tendons considerably.

On one occasion I was riding with a friend and we approached a break-water we regularly jumped. We were talking and it was only at the last minute I saw that all the sand had been washed away by the last tide leaving a heap of broken rubble beneath. I shouted a warning and managed to swerve my horse away from take off but my friend was not so lucky and both he and his horse had a nasty fall.

It also shames me to recall that, when first living near the sea, I rode out one day without checking the scene. It was a cold blustery winter's day and on that occasion the jumps were quite minimal and the last one high. As we leapt over I saw to my horror that there were two people huddled together beneath us on the sand. I don't know who was the most horrified, them or us!

One of my riders who had not checked the jumps at all galloped towards breakwaters so fast he did not notice a protruding bolt which pierced the knee of the mare as she jumped. He continued to gallop on until someone shouted to him to stop as the leg was bleeding badly. It is always best to err on the cautious side and check and double check the conditions.

Riding with Others

Riding in company always needs extra vigilance. Some horses, and their riders, become so excited that they throw caution to the winds at the expense of everybody else. It is vital to be aware at all times of what is going on around you.

No one enjoys another car sitting on their bumper when driving and it is the same with riding. You will only have yourself to blame if your horse is kicked when riding too close to another. Keep your distance both in front, behind and sideways.

Sometimes it can be necessary to get out of the way. A loose horse or one out of control can be hazardous. Be sure you don't suddenly change direction for no reason, especially when jumping.

Jumping in company

Good manners are a prerequisite when jumping in company. (see chapter 7 on cross country riding) Apart from being rude, it is downright dangerous to overtake when approaching a fence. Queue barging is unforgivable.

If your horse refuses at an obstacle, do let others go before you try again. It is very frustrating having to keep an enthusiastic horse waiting while another keeps steadfastly refusing.

Don't ever cut across any one approaching a fence and when jumping an obstacle remember to ride clear when landing as there may be someone following on close behind.

If there are children on the ride, do keep an eye out for them. They certainly do not have your experience and so you need to be ready for anything!

Courtesy Check List

✔   DO remember that anything can happen. This is one of the reasons why riding is exciting.

✔   DO be aware of other people and be polite at all times.

✔   DO dress correctly and for safety.

✗   DON'T give indeterminate signals. Be clear.

✗   DON'T ride out bareback and with only a headcollar in public places.

✗   DON'T give anyone a reason for criticising horse riders.

✗   DON'T ride on private land without permission.

✗   DON'T forget that some folk are frightened of horses, so keep your distance and your horse under control.

2

Buying and Selling

There is no secret so close as that
between a rider and his horse.

R.S.Surtees (1805-64)

BUYING

For most people who enjoy riding the ultimate goal is to own their own horse. He will always be there for you, close at hand, hopefully, ready to be ridden whenever you feel like it: someone to tell all your troubles to while out hacking in idyllic surroundings.

Seeking out your perfect partner can be a less than perfect experience, but if you give the exercise some careful thought beforehand it could prove pleasant, even exciting, and not as fraught with difficulties as others would have you believe.

There will always be those friends and acquaintances quick to fill you in with details of their horrendous experiences before they found Ginger or Dobbin, but ignore their cries of doom and set about your search with enthusiasm.

If you ride for pleasure, you will need an animal with a good temperament who is willing to please and who is 'well put together'. This means that he will be able to perform more easily and be more likely to stay sound.

Ask the first-time buyer what kind of animal they are looking for and you will usually receive very descriptive answers: 'It must be a chestnut'; 'I wouldn't entertain a horse that was not a Thoroughbred'; 'It has to be an Arab'; 'A good jumper is essential', and so on.

Several points arise here. Obviously, choosing on colour alone would be very foolish indeed, and it goes without saying that Arabs are known for their speed, as well as their endurance, so that they benefit from experienced, sensitive riders. Thoroughbreds are best left in the hands of well established horsemen and women and a good jumper needs a rider who is a confident, capable jumper also to keep up his enthusiasm.

Hearing such answers always reminds me of teenagers discussing the necessary qualities of the people they hope to marry. The perfect man must be six feet tall with black hair and love the theatre. To everyone's surprise the lady chooses a short, stocky man who loves football, and her, so that is a success. Similarly, a young man hankers after a petite blonde who loves cooking. To the amusement of his friends he marries a six foot lady who is very good at ordering take-aways – but loves him. Another success story. It is just the same with finding the right horse. Looks don't matter one little bit if you are riding for pleasure and don't really want to cut a dash in the show ring. It is the compatibility which counts. Each suiting the other.

Looks don't matter

When you are a riding teacher, clients always expect you to find exactly the right horse for them. I have travelled many miles in search of the ideal mount but remember two cases very well. Parents with high expectations are the ones to beware of! One little girl had started lessons reluctantly under pressure from her father. She was not particularly keen on the riding part, preferring to pat the ponies and bring them carrots. In an ideal world she could have helped a friend look after a pony and gained confidence that way. However, after a short period of weekly lessons she was gaining confidence but had not captured the art of rising to the trot and, indeed, was still on the leading rein. There was nothing else for it, said father, she needs her own pony and she will progress in leaps and bounds (literally I thought !).

So off we went on a pony hunt. Out of six ponies seen in two counties, there were only two I suggested we kept well away from. One good natured pony was susceptible to laminitis and the other 13hh variety, a magnificent looking show pony, was so enthusiastic and on-going that I was hard put to hold it when test riding. Any one of the remaining four would have been ideal.

Two days later the father phoned to say he had bought the laminitic pony *and* the show specimen. Some weeks passed before the first was shut in the stable with a severe bout of laminitis and the poor child had broken her ribs falling off the speed merchant.

The second nightmare scenario concerned a tall, middle-aged man who had just taken up riding and his tiny four-foot something sister who had joined him on his lessons but was very nervous. His enthusiasm caused him to look for a horse to buy far too soon in their new equestrian hobby. They wanted to share a horse but, in vain, I tried to explain the constraints of their different sizes and expectations. While he was extremely daredevil in his approach, his sister was the opposite, being very apprehensive.

We travelled three counties looking for their beast. I knew what I was searching for, a good natured horse who had been everywhere, done everything, was a decent age and loved people. Indeed, the horse everyone is looking for!

I suggested visiting a reputable dealer who sold to show jumpers but usually had a variety of other horses as well. (If you decide to use the services of a dealer make sure it is one with a good reputation in the horse world).

One particularly pretty black 15 hh Thoroughbred caught their eye and I agreed to try her out. She certainly was not suitable for them. For one thing she was too small for the gentleman and I suspected, rightly as it proved, that she was too fast for his sister. The mare was young, but anxious to please, and I thought she would make someone a very attractive dressage mount. She also had a scopey jump.

In the third county we found Hercules. He had to be, possibly, the ugliest horse I had ever seen with a huge Roman nose and thick set body. However, his ears and his eyes were huge and so was his heart. He loved people and he took me round a cross country course which included a huge, solid, flat topped table which he jumped with ease. It was, apparently, his favourite jump and nothing to do with my skill! He cantered obligingly with the gentleman and trotted sedately with his sister. He was ideal.

They rang me at the week-end. They had bought the little Thoroughbred and would I keep her at livery? She stayed for some months until they decided to keep her at home. Overfed and under exercised she bolted one day and the lady fell off injuring herself quite badly. The horse was quickly sold and that was the end of their riding enthusiasm. It is all so sad when people don't take notice of expert knowledge. So surely the moral must be, that if you pay for advice make sure you take heed of it and don't throw your money away.

A Word of Warning

Horse trading has always attracted a devious use of language. Do not expect everyone to be as honest as you are. I was once sold a Thoroughbred by a girl who said she had lost interest. This was a euphemism for 'lost her nerve'. She failed to tell me that her horse could gallop backwards almost as fast as it could go forward and that it had once bolted on a major road, jumping a Mini car in the process. I suppose this could well be advertised as proven jumping potential!

Another well worn-theme is to be told a horse is nine years old. Many people want a horse who is experienced and has been around and assume that by this age he has gained some knowledge. This is all very well in theory but it could be that the owner has lost interest and the horse has been standing in field and stable for the past two or three years. Always ask around for local knowledge when buying.

Unfortunately, after the age of nine, it is difficult to tell a hor\. by his teeth, so while there are other factors involved, the 'nine ye could be nineteen !

Of course, the ideal situation is to buy a horse you know, but this does not happen as often as we would like. It is not a good idea to buy a horse you have only seen and admired from afar ridden by others. Unless they are well established old plods, horses react differently to different riders. Also, seeing a horse out will not give you a clue as to his behaviour at home and in the stable.

Incidentally, if you are visiting a fair especially an Irish fair, in the hope of finding your ideal mount, it is considered bad form to ask a seller, 'How much?' and then walk away without further ado. Banter and barter is the name of the game here. (This method of purchase is not for the inexperienced !).

Golden Rules

Ask questions. Does the horse get on with other horses, mares and geldings, and other animals, such as donkeys and dogs? Is he well mannered when out ridden with other horses? Is he traffic proof? Good to shoe, box, clip and groom? Could he live alone if necessary? Does he live out most of the time or is he stabled? Will he be a liability if not ridden every day? Ask another horse owner to help you compile a list of questions relevant to your lifestyle.

Decide on your price limit and stick to it. If the vendor is adamant about keeping to the asking price and you can't afford it, you will be wasting both your time by visiting to look. Don't overreach yourself financially or by ability. The horse may well have the potential for international stardom, but do you? Even if you can afford it and have the money ready, it really is not fair to buy an advanced horse and stick a beginner on top. In truth, it could be lethal.

Before you make arrangements to see the horse, always insist that should you like the horse, you intend to use the services of your own vet to check the animal over. If the seller is not happy with this arrangement it may be right to be suspicious and look elsewhere.

Good manners extend especially to making arrangements to view. Always keep the appointment. We all lead busy lives and it is extremely irritating to spend all morning grooming for a prospective buyer who fails to show. If you find you are running late, give the seller a quick call to update your plans. If, for some unforeseen reason you are not going to be able to keep the appointment do give them the courtesy of knowing that you will not be turning up.

If they can only be available on Saturday or Sunday for you to view the horse, then so be it. If they want cash when the deal has been arranged, then take cash. Remember, it is the vendor who is calling the tune here. The amount of deposit requested can be variable. Some ask for a token £100, others may want 10 percent and so on. If the potential buyer changes his mind after giving a deposit for reasons other than the bad result of a veterinary report, he loses the deposit.

The current owner may make claims about the horse's bloodline, but it is quite in order to ask to see the relevant papers. A genuine seller will be only too happy to show them to you and discuss the breeding.

When buying, do not be a time-waster. From the seller's point of view there is nothing worse than setting aside precious time to present a horse at its best for 'purchasers' who are basically out for a drive in the country with a free ride at the end of it. Phrases such as 'Of course, we have to sell our pony first,' or 'My husband has to get his new car before we could actually think of buying another horse', spring to mind.

As a matter of courtesy the buyer should give his telephone number to the seller in case the horse is sold quickly, or in case of emergency. Do not believe folk who tell you to arrive before the appointed viewing time. Not only is it exceedingly rude, it is also a time-wasting exercise. The chances are you will see everything necessary anyway.

If visiting an equestrian establishment, perhaps a stud or riding school, do not wander everywhere poking about and looking in all the boxes without asking first. Seeking permission to view does not cost anything and you will be thought of more highly if you ask first and look later.

If you have made up your mind that the horse is not suitable, say so at once. If, on the other hand, you have decided to investigate further be sure to get the seller to ride him first and watch carefully. When it is your turn to ride, on no account try to get the horse to misbehave by getting hold of his head or kicking.

For a successful conclusion to buying a horse perhaps the two most important people to consider are your vet, to check the animal's health and an expert rider to assess the horse's capabilities with regard to your current level of riding.

Whether the 'consultant' comes with you on the initial trip, or if first impressions are promising, on a second visit, it is good manners to: a) advise the vendor of your intention to bring a 'consultant' and b) at least offer to pay for the expert's time.

Some vets offer two levels of service: a basic check over and one which is much more thorough. I would always recommend choosing the more expensive option for both your peace of mind and your pocket in the long run! A horse with medical problems can cost you a fortune. Added to this, any future insurance claims may be assisted if a full vet's certificate from time of purchase is available.

Courtesy Check List
Buying

✔ DO ask your vet to check over any possible purchase before you get too excited.

✔ DO decide on your price range and keep within your limit.

✔ DO treat the seller as you would expect to be treated in the same circumstances.

✔ DO ride the horse and handle him to see if you 'gel'.

✘ DON'T ask a friend who is not an expert to go with you for advice. This is time for the experts.

✘ DON'T insult the sellers by trying to knock them down on price to a ridiculous degree.

✘ DON'T make arrangements to view and not turn up.

✘ DON'T choose a horse whose achievements are much greater than yours. He will only be confused or frighten you to death!

✘ DON'T buy an unbroken three year old because he is cheap unless you are very experienced at making horses. (Monty Roberts uses

the term 'making horses' instead of the unfortunate phrase 'break
ing horses') and one who has not been 'made with care' is very
difficult to put right.

SELLING

Selling a horse is usually a disturbing experience and I think that before
the completion of the sale it is quite in order to request a visit to the
potential new owner's home to see the facilities on offer for your horse.
Most people are only too pleased to show you the effort they have put in
to welcome him into their lives.

Generally speaking, horse owners are realistic about their horse's value;
but if he is a special friend and for sale through no fault of his own, the
seller will only want the best for him and if a super home were on offer
with people who would love and care for him in every way, the seller
might drop the price if necessary. However, a word of warning. Do not
let your horse go out on loan to a would-be buyer.

Horses are far too valuable in terms of emotions and finance to go off
on holiday to people we do not know. I say this with much feeling. Give
as many possibilities of contact and riding as wanted; but don't let your
horse out of your sight.

I had always kept to this maxim until a member of the aristocracy
approached me with a view to loaning a horse for their daughter before
buying. I decided it would be churlish not to let the horse go to what I
fondly imagined were improved conditions to the luxury provided
at home.

The horse was away for the Easter holidays. Regular telephone calls
established that the daughter loved her and the mare was evented, took
part in Pony Club activities and everything else – and was returned one
breakfast time as unsuitable. No explanation was forthcoming from the
groom who delivered her back most apologetically. Later we learned she
had been kept down some steps in a small stable which could almost be
described as a coal hole, a far cry from her large loose box at home. She
had been twitched for grooming and clipping (for speed of action) and
it was a long time before we got her round to her usual self again.

Another section of the horsy community to beware of is that core
which comes ostensibly to buy, but in reality to have an afternoon's free
riding at the expense of your poor horse. After performing a faultless

dressage test, jumping a course and galloping until you shouted 'Enough!' he will retire to his stable absolutely shattered and you will never hear from them again. There will be times when you feel your courteous side may be wearing a bit thin!

Try not to present a false picture

Put as much information in the advertisement as possible to avoid time wasters and talk to potential buyers at length before they visit. If they have to travel a long way it could save their time and yours if you fill them in with as much detail as necessary. It is a good idea to get copies of your horse's best photographs so that you can send them to prospective buyers who live far away and videos will give them an even a better idea as to whether this is the type of horse they are looking for. Be honest. Tell them about his foibles, allergies, quirky habits and so on. It can only benefit your horse in the long run. Try to think of everything that his new owners would need to know for his comfort and well-being. If the horse is high withered or has a special bit and bridle, it would be both sensible and kind to sell the tack at the same time.

It is essential to have the horse correctly measured before selling. Wrong measurement can mean elimination from classes for wrong height, giving huge disappointment to the rider. 15.1 hh does not mean 14.2 hh and you won't get away with it.

If your horse has a fizzy temperament, don't wear him out before the unsuspecting buyers arrive hoping to present a calm well-behaved animal. They would find out soon enough and, anyway, there are plenty of riders who prefer a bit of sparkle in a horse.

Courtesy check list
Selling

✔ DO include as much information as you can afford in the initial advertisement.

✔ DO sell any special tack with the horse.

✔ DO be honest about the animal's health and behaviour.

✔ DO have him professionally measured.

✔ DO be aware that some people will feel the need to try your horse more than once and (if you are happy that they are serious) make provision for this.

✖ DON'T present a false picture of your horse in the hope of a sale.

✖ DON'T keep quiet on anything they should know about. If he tends to kick when being groomed or if he doesn't like pigs, they should be warned.

Does Size Matter?

In small proportions we just beauty see;
Ben Jonson c.1573-1637

Unfortunately there are some snobs in the horse world, especially those who look down on adults who choose to ride ponies. If the person is not too heavy and the mount is up to weight I have never seen it as a problem. However, you must remember that although you may weigh only 8 stone unclothed on the bathroom scales, when your riding clothes, hat, boots and the tack are added to the equation, it can make it considerably more.

Obviously if your first pony was 11 hh and you are now tall and gangly, you would only look foolish and both you and your pony would be very uncomfortable. On the other hand, a fit cob of 13 hh is well able to carry a lightweight adult. Common sense should play a large part in this debate.

It does seem hard, when you have had a pony since childhood, that on reaching a certain age you are expected to say goodbye to him and set about choosing a horse. If your legs are not too long and you are not too heavy for him, why not continue with the animal you love? It certainly seems more sensible than choosing the heartbreak of perhaps having to sell your companion in order to buy a larger model you don't know.

A friend of mine kept her pony at a livery yard and on her first morning with her foot in the stirrup someone burst out laughing and said, 'Surely you are not going to ride THAT?' Where is the problem? In past times Dartmoor ponies were ridden and raced by men as well as being used for transport and shepherding, while today they are still used for trekking.

Under-horsed or perfectly ponied?

Some people ride horses and others ride ponies. Instead of this being an amicable situation, when adults are involved there is invariably friction. While I was editing *Today's Horse*, a national equestrian magazine, we ran a debate on the subject which went on for months. Although the pony riders explained they only rode animals who were up to their weight it still caused animosity.

It started with a letter from a young mother who rode a 13.2hh gelding. She said she was barred from serious ridden classes and had to use the services of a child rider for these. She therefore limited herself to Best Turned Out, Best Rider and showing in hand. She complained that she was always considered a joke though her mount was treated exactly the same as a horse and, that at 10 stone, she did not consider her weight to be a problem.

She was even mocked when out hacking. People walking their dogs would ask if she was riding her child's pony and it was worse when competing. When a county-level judge heard they had completed a seven-mile paper hunt, his reply was that the pony must have been on its knees at the end and suggested that she was slightly under-horsed. This particular pony was capable of carrying the weight and was a real handful to ride, so really would not have been suitable as a child's pony.

The letter writer begged horse owners not to look down on adults who preferred to ride ponies and certainly not to underestimate them. She advised pony riders to be proud of their mounts and not to be afraid of what others might say.

Correspondence poured in by the sackload. Experts agreed that many of the larger riding ponies, as well as most of the heavier Mountain and Moorland breeds were more than capable of carrying adults. Fells and Highlands can carry up to 13 stone. Very often a 14hh native pony will be able to carry more weight than a 15.2hh Thoroughbred.

In her article, 'Pony People', Helen Deverill suggested that smaller adults could look more suitably mounted on a pony than a horse and that, for those of mature years, a pony could feel safer as you are closer to the ground! It was generally acknowledged that ponies were both cheaper to buy and to keep as they could be kept out all year.

It is true that some serious equestrians tend to mock pony people and a little more thought and courtesy could go a long way towards healing the breach. Remember Stroller, a 14.2 hh pony? No one ever mocked

Marion Mould or her mount when they won a silver medal at the Olympics in 1968, he then taking her on to be European Ladies' Champion in 1970.

An age limit of 16 years for 14.2hh and under seems unnecessarily restrictive. Adults who prefer to ride ponies should not be treated as inferior or second class riders. Show organisers are always struggling to meet costs. Perhaps if they were to include classes for ponies with adult riders in their schedules they might be surprised at the response. Adult pony riders are accepted in native showing classes and endurance riding, so why not others?

Courtesy Check List

✓   DO keep a constant check on your weight to make sure you are not going over the top!

✓   DO treat pony riders with the same respect given to horse riders.

✓   DO remember that years ago ponies were the only mode of transport for many isolated communities and that adults rode them all the time.

✖   DON'T forget that many pony breeds were originally used as pack animals, to carry adults and that larger breeds – such as Welsh Section D, Dales, Highlands and Haflingers are well up to this task.

✖   DON'T forget you could be better off financially by keeping a pony rather than a horse.

✖   DON'T mock those who prefer ponies. If there is no cruelty involved it is, after all, purely a matter of choice.

Keeping a Horse at Livery

Its special aim being to induce kindness, sympathy, and an understanding treatment of horses:

Anna Sewell (1871)

The sentiments expressed by Anna Sewell on her reasons for writing Black Beauty are those we are looking for when choosing a livery yard for our horse. The welfare of the horse is paramount.

If you have a horse or pony at livery, the most courteous way to behave towards the proprietor of the yard is to do what you are asked. He may be *your* horse, but he is living on someone else's premises and whilst in his or her care, the *knowledgeable* livery owner should have the last word.

Unfortunately, some owners think they are entitled to do as they please about the place because they are paying for their horse's keep but, naturally, they need to remember they are keeping their animal on someone else's property and should behave accordingly.

If your horse is being kept at a riding school, having a working livery scheme might seem an attractive proposition economically. However, paying a reduced fee in return for your horse being ridden by other people rarely works to your advantage. You will have no say in who rides your horse. Beginners will inhibit his progress, but you could not reasonably object. The weekends are popular times and this would probably be your riding time also. Before agreeing to this system a lot of thought needs to be given to a satisfactory arrangement.

It would not be sensible to turn your horse out without asking. Some premises keep mares and geldings separate and horses are like people. Some get on better with different horses and ponies and are turned out accordingly. There may well be a rota of turn-outs and it is up to you to learn the system. The same applies to mucking out. It is essential to adhere to the status quo for all concerned.

It is always polite to ask permission before doing anything on the premises. You may think it would be an excellent idea to fix a saddle bracket on to the wall outside your stable. Don't even think about doing it before asking if it would be acceptable. It might prove to be an eyesore, it might be in the way when sweeping the yard; there may be other reasons you have not considered.

Similarly, don't help yourself to manure from the muck heap without asking. In most yards the heap is a beautifully kept square structure where some is 'on the make' and the rest well rotted and ready to sell. You will not be popular if you dig away leaving an awful mess for someone else to clear up. It doesn't cost anything to ask and it will save misunderstandings.

Do not disturb

In good yards, there are always sound reasons for the rules laid down. Sometimes owners are requested not to visit the yard after a certain time. It is a thoughtless person who takes a 'goodnight carrot' to their horse after he has been left to sleep. Once horses have been fed for the night they should be left in peace.

When John Lassetter was in charge of the Porlock Vale Equitation Centre in Somerset, there was a notice over his beloved Lippizaners proclaiming 'Horses Resting. Do Not Disturb' and woe betide anyone who ignored the sign when visiting in the afternoon!

As a former livery yard owner, I remember one occasion when an owner arrived late one evening without notice and took her animal out of the loose box wearing headcollar and rope and proceeded to put her young child on top (no saddle, no riding hat).

She then ran the horse trotting round the yard, arousing the interest of the other horses and myself. When admonished for her lack of safety precautions and thought for the other animals she was very angry indeed; declaring that what she did with her horse and her child was her business. Incidents like this do not bode well for amicable relationships.

Another prospective client announced she was not prepared to wear a riding hat and so lost a place at the stables. If horse owners are truly interested in the welfare of their animals, they will read all they can on the subject and be happy to listen to the opinions of those with years of horse keeping experience behind them. This knowledge will be invaluable to those who intend looking after their animals at home one day.

Communication

Communication is not only a matter of courtesy between horse owner, yard owner and staff ; it is absolutely vital. When making initial enquiries always be honest, especially about your horse. If he weaves, windsucks or is a crib-biter, own up to it at the initial interview. If he is aggressive towards other horses in the field, say so. That way you could be helped with possible solutions and at least you will then know how the yard owner feels about it This is so much better than being asked to leave because the other horses and owners are being upset.

If you intend going on a half-day ride, or being out longer than usual, do inform the staff so they don't send a search party looking for you.

Having an away-day

Always keep the owner informed of your plans and ring at the specified times. Mobile telephones can be a boon but, not everyone working on a yard has one to hand and if not, it is frustrating to keep running from house to stables and back to convey messages.

Suppose you intend riding at 6 a.m. and you know the horses are not fed until 7.30 a.m.? A telephone call to see if an earlier feed could be arranged would be sensible or perhaps extra hay could be supplied the night before. Don't ever ride less than an hour after a short feed. Riders who expect to ride without leaving the animal sufficient time to digest his food are a real trial. After all, it will be the livery owner left with the job of calling the vet to a case of colic. The owner will be long gone!

If you have requested your horse be groomed for 10 a.m. then be there at that time. If you are late the horse will probably be tied up, bored with waiting, or, at worst, let loose again to roll and get dirty. Straw and shavings in a tail always ruin the final appearance.

If you decide to move your horse elsewhere, give the owners of the stable as much notice as possible. They may have a waiting list which sets up a chain reaction. One owner sent two strangers up to the yard where the horse was kept to lead the horse to a new home rather than tell the owner of his plans. Naturally, staff accosted the strangers going into the stable and were upset at the discourteous way the situation was handled.

While on the subject of strangers, don't tell all your friends they can ride your horse any time. If the staff see someone they don't know approaching your stable they are bound to be suspicious. So, make a point of introducing them and making formal arrangements when necessary but, do remember, it will be your responsibility if anything goes wrong.

Consideration

Owners don't always realise the attachment formed by staff to their charges. Stable management is intensive daily work and the constant attention demanded by horses means close contact with the workers. It is usually upsetting for them when one leaves, but always exciting when a new horse arrives. Therefore it is in your interests, and that of your horse, to treat his groom kindly.

On the other side of the coin, make sure that the grooms and yard staff treat your horse with kindness. Writing twenty-three centuries ago, the great Greek horseman Xenophon stated, 'The one great precept and practice in using a horse is this, never deal with him when you are in a fit of passion. A fit of passion is a thing that has no foresight in it, and so we often have to rue the day when we gave way to it'. Naturally, this applies also when we are riding.

Perhaps the most important consideration for the client is to remember that livery owners are, on the whole, dedicated and very busy people so it is kind to make allowances. I will never forget, some years ago, a lovely lady whose life was totally consumed by the horses and ponies in her care. In the frantic arrangements necessary for getting children and their ponies to go hunting, she organised everything successfully but forgot to take a horse for herself and her assistant was dispatched back to the stables for the beast!

Remember that the yard owner has to pay for all the feed and bedding in bulk involving large sums of money, so be sure to pay your bills promptly. You would not be pleased if the hay and short feed were not forthcoming when needed, so save the embarrassment of being asked for money.

Finally, a word of advice to those whose horse is stable-kept, whether at home or elsewhere. His stable or loose box is his private sanctuary where he feels perfectly safe and relaxed. Don't suddenly appear at the doorway or open the door without any warning. If he is sleeping, or miles away mentally, he will jump out of his skin. Always speak to him on your approach to let him know something is about to happen.

Courtesy Check List

✓   DO respect the yard owner's wishes and rules.

✓   DO remember the importance of safety at all times. (Be sure not to put yourself, friends, family or your horse in a dangerous situation on the yard or anywhere else).

✓   DO keep in constant touch with the yard owner and staff.

✓   DO be aware of your horse's needs and those of the people looking after him.

✓   DO treat your groom with the respect and kindness due.

✖   DON'T leave bits of baler twine lying around for a person to trip over or a horse to get his foot caught. Baler twine does not easily break and can be a real hazard.

✖   DON'T fling your headcollar and rope down when you have finished. Hang it up wherever it is supposed to go.

✖   DON'T decide to shampoo your horse outside the stables when the others are supposed to be resting. (It may well be your day off, but choose your moment without inconveniencing others).

✖   DON'T pick your horse's feet out on the yard and leave the bits lying there. Pick the feet out into a skip and then throw the mud and debris away.

✖ DON'T leave plastic bags where dogs and horses can get at them. They can be fatal when eaten.

✖ DON'T take your dog up to the yard to cause mayhem while you see to your horse. It may well be saving you time on exercising, but it is certainly not fair on the resident dogs or anyone else.

The Yard Owner's Viewpoint

When initial inquiries are made by a prospective client, do make sure you explain the items they are expected to provide. Yards differ in their requirements. Some expect feed bowls and water buckets to be provided as well as headcollars and ropes.

Make sure the worming system is clear. Who does it, when and how often? An owner does not want to give a horse a wormer only to find that the animal has been given one earlier in the day. One of you needs

Not a good idea !

to keep a record of dates of worming, vaccinations, and shoeing. Point out the importance of insurance for horses at livery.

Most full livery yards use one farrier for all the horses. It could be confusing and disruptive to have several attending the same premises, so be clear at the beginning.

Consistency is essential. Don't have someone groom a horse ready for a ride on one occasion and not have time to do it on another occasion. Clients need to know where they stand, so putting down ground rules right from the start is only fair to both sides.

As a yard owner, probably the most important piece of knowledge I gained very quickly is that, without exception, both men and women are extremely touchy about their animals and criticism, however constructive, is not kindly accepted. It is essential to realise that each horse is the best equine ever to trot up the drive.

Once you have mastered this maxim you will know that where questions need to be asked or hints given, treading softly is the answer. 'Perhaps you should... ' or 'Have you considered... ', 'I knew a horse once...' etc. not, 'Well, if you will insist on feeding oats, what can you expect?' Another idea could be to suggest, tactfully, trying an alternative diet, pointing out this can alter a horse's behaviour.

Sometimes it is apparent to the stable owner that the reason for the horse's uncoordinated way of going is the lack of expertise on the part of the rider. Now this is a tricky one. Some people don't take kindly to the suggestion that professional instruction might be needed. Mentioning the name of a reputable instructor during conversation or discussing the merits of a rider who is doing well and was trained by X could be a satisfactory ploy. Luckily, most realise their inadequacies and are only too happy to seek help in becoming more proficient, for their sakes and that of their horses.

Finally, having a written contract is a good idea from the point of view of both parties, as they cover most eventualities, especially important arrangements, such as the procedures for calling the vet if the horse is seriously ill or fatally injured.

Courtesy Check List
Yard Owner

✓   DO start off on the right foot by giving each client a copy of the contract and/or a typed list of rules for the yard. Request they read them carefully and query anything they are not happy about BEFORE they move their horse in.

✓   DO remember that communication is a two way process.If you are going away, inform your clients of the details of those taking your place, how long you will be gone and give dates.

✓   DO be sure the financial arrangements are clear: monthly or weekly payments and the systems for buying wormers and paying for the farrier and the vet when necessary.

✓   DO give plenty of notice if you are going to raise the charges. It would be unkind to announce suddenly, 'Oh, by the way, livery goes up by a fiver next time.' Many owners struggle financially to keep their horses and rises are a necessary nightmare to be arranged in advance.

✖   DON'T treat your clients as if they were children.

✖   DON'T ever make comparisons between people or horses.

✖   DON'T talk in glowing terms of the client who had the box before.

✖   DON'T brag about your previous riding prowess. A tack room lined with photographs and rosettes of clients is fine. Personal triumphs could well be intimidating and might be better kept in the home.

It's Good to Talk

She's not very tall, that's plain to see,
      Up to my nose I should think.
She's sometimes tired. Is it me?
      Carrying the water for me to drink.

My stable is clean. I give you that.
      And the food? Well, I can't complain;
But the hours I spend in that there stall
      Listening to the rain.

It's the fields I want and I'm sure she's aware;
      She knows as well as me.
When I jump in the air and roll on my back
      She's always there to see.

Horses and humans. Guess we're the same,
      Longing for fields anew.
But I suppose there are always 'ifs' and 'buts'
      And other things to do.

George Cadden

Cherish Your Farrier

No foot: no horse

ANON

No foot, no horse is a good maxim to remember. So, if you have a good farrier, treat him like gold dust, with care! It is in his interest to be polite to you and kind to your horse. He should be efficient and work in conjunction with a vet and you should be grateful for his services in what is, after all, a back-breaking task.

I think you should always make allowances for his time-keeping. Horses are unpredictable creatures and a fidgety horse takes longer to shoe than a quiet, well mannered animal which can make him late for his next appointment. A reliable farrier will let you know if he has to change his time substantially.

They don't ask for much, these supermen. They are usually obliged when you are there at the appointed time holding the horse with head-collar and rope, standing on a firm, hard surface with his feet already picked out. He will not be pleased if he has to wait:

a) for you to get ready, looking for your wellies and coat nor;

b) for you to go into the field and try to catch your horse.

He will also be unhappy if you present him with a horse with wet, muddy legs to hold: another reason for having your horse well prepared in advance. Like all professionals, a farrier's time is valuable and not to be wasted.

Some farriers like trimming or shoeing outside, some prefer to be in. If he is an 'outside' man be sure your animal will stand and be tied or held happily and calmly outside. Practise in good weather by grooming him outdoors so that he gets used to the situation.

If working inside, bedding should be taken up in the stable or loose box so the horse can stand square. Holding a foot up to trim is all very well but the farrier needs to see the animal standing on all four feet to assess for the correct shape.

Make sure there are no droppings. He does not want to step backwards into a pile of manure at a tricky moment, or indeed, at any time. Keep a shovel and skip outside the stable door at the ready lest there should be an accident.

Think Ahead

A well mannered horse can be shod twice as quickly as one who messes about, so pick your horse's feet up often and make him used to being handled in the stable. It is a good idea to have plenty of male visitors to the yard. Horses owned and cared for by women can be very touchy about the opposite sex and there are not yet enough lady farriers or vets to redress the balance.

You will not be a popular client if you leave your horse's feet for three

You should be the person ready and waiting – not the farrier

months and then telephone, panic-stricken, asking for a visit right away as your horse has gone lame. The farrier will not be fooled by a rider who rings to say the horse is lame and needs attention when what they really mean is that they either forgot, or left it too late to book in, and now they want to ride.

Don't telephone on a Thursday expecting a visit the same week. It is also worth remembering that a farrier *always* knows his own work and he will know instantly if you have used the services of other farriers in between times. Plan your visits ahead so the farrier can organise his diary too.

If you are unable to be there when the farrier comes, do make sure there will be a responsible, horsey person who knows the horse taking your place.

Be sure to pay each time he visits. Time is money and the horse and the money should be ready and waiting for him. Debts have a horrible way of mounting up and it will sour your relationship to owe money.

If you keep your horse at home it goes without saying that a mug of tea or coffee is usually much appreciated. Owners who come outside carrying and drinking a cup of tea to watch the work being done but not offering the same are not popular people! The favourites are those who offer soap and a towel as well as tea or coffee. Trimming and shoeing is hard, physical work needing skill and dedication. It is to your advantage to treat your farrier well. He does not have to come out to you.

Courtesy Check List

✓   DO be ready at the arranged time with a clean, calm horse.

✓   DO be prepared to ask a friend to hold your horse during the daytime if you cannot be there. Not all horses tie up happily if no-one familiar is around.

✓   DO pay when the work is done.

✘   DON'T call the farrier the night before you want him to come.

✘   DON'T ask him to come in the evening after a hard day's work: his day has to finish sometime.

✖   DON'T have your horse's feet and legs covered in mud, straw or anything else for the visit.

✖   DON'T oil or grease the feet beforehand. It jams up the tools and the feet slip out of his hand making it extremely difficult to work.

✖   DON'T refer to your farrier as a blacksmith. Although the two professions work in the same medium, your farrier goes through extremely vigorous and specific training before he is qualified to shoe your horse

Dressage – Equestrian Ballet

Grace under Pressure

Ernest Hemingway (1899 – 1961)

It is no wonder that spectators watching dressage for the first time liken the movements to horses dancing. The elegance can be breathtaking, giving people pause for thought as to how this is achieved.

The very word 'dressage' has always been surrounded by an air of mystique, especially to those starting riding. Perhaps it is the pronunciation, or the fact that it is a French word that gives it this aura.

However, the translation of dressage is only preparation, or a form of training, and most horses should be able to perform basic dressage movements for their own good and that of their riders.

This method of training a horse to perform manoeuvres in response to the rider's body signals has many followers, both as a sport in its own right and is, of course, an important part of horse trials.

Any horse can be trained for dressage; but some may not have the capacity for Grand Prix excellence and you may have to settle for less. Professional trainers will tell you how disappointing it is that riders nearly always contact them to ask for help with their *horse*. Very rarely do they consider any fault may lie with their riding. Think carefully before you blame the horse for wrong doing. It is no good buying a splendidly schooled animal unless you are up to the job of riding as well as, or better than, the rider who owned him before.

If you decide to compete at dressage, enter at a level below, not above the capabilities of you and your horse so that you shine, rather than struggle. Don't annoy the judge by presenting a horse who is not ready for the test entered. You are only wasting everyone's time, including your own, and over-facing your animal – a good way of putting him off dressage forever!

Find a test suitable for your horse's capabilities

See that your horse's flu vaccination is up to date as some shows ask to see a valid certificate before you can compete.

Don't have him shod the day before, he might be a bit clumsy. About a week beforehand would be ideal.

Dress is important in a dressage test. You and your animal must be as smart and presentable as possible to catch the judge's eye.

Your mount needs a simple snaffle bridle for a preliminary level test, but you will need to check carefully to see which bits and nosebands are allowed for various competitions.

A white numnah is smart, definitely not coloured, but black can be used on a grey horse. Fancy coloured girths, browbands and reins are quite wrong and there must be no bandages, boots or martingales on the horse since these will result in elimination from the competition.

As far as you are concerned, gloves are as necessary as the hat. Hair must be neat, preferably in a hair net. Tweed coats are correct for a preliminary level test, with a sober shirt and tie, or hunting stock and pin. White stocks are only worn with navy or black coats and button-holes are never worn.

Jewellery is frowned upon unless it is so discreet as to be almost invisible, so what is the point of wearing any? The same applies to ladies' make-up.

Give yourself enough time to have your equipment checked, and to ride in quietly. As your time to compete gets nearer, try to be working in the proximity of the arena, so that your arena steward can see where you are and can direct you towards the arena with the minimum amount of fuss or time loss when it is your turn to compete.

Before the test, check the signal used to start the test and remember to show your number to the judge's writer.

A simple salute at X is all that is needed in tests which have an initial halt. Now that many people wear hats with chin straps it is no longer necessary for a man to take off his hat when saluting. When the horse is settled in halt, look at the judge and smile in a friendly manner. Put reins and whip (if carrying one) in your left hand, drop the right hand down by your right hip with the back of your hand facing the judge, with fingers pointing downward. Nod your head slowly and then back again. Without rushing, put your right hand back on the rein, count to three and move off.

After the test, when you have left the arena at free walk on a long rein at A, make much of your horse and walk him until he is cool and relaxed. See to his comfort before your own. Even if you were not a winner it is polite to attend the prize giving and, of course, thank the secretary/organiser before leaving for home.

Whatever the outcome, take your test sheet home and study the marks and remarks ready for the next time.

Courtesy Check List

✓ DO plan carefully and decide how much riding-in time you will need, then add 10 minutes in case any thing goes awry.

✓ DO learn the test fully. Not all tests will be commanded, but, if you are going to use the services of a caller, it is helpful to be acquainted with the test.

✓　DO be sure to switch off from the world completely when you enter the ring, thinking only of the task ahead. **Mind over matter is important in every aspect of horsemanship.**

✓　DO choose a test that is well within the capabilities of your horse. It is better to shine at preliminary level than make a nonsense of a novice or elementary test.

✓　DO keep your cool if things are not going to your satisfaction.

✘　DON'T look at others to see how they are doing. They are not the ones that matter. Just use all your concentration on what you are doing.

✘　DON'T over work your horse. Work quietly as if you were at home, neither over emphasising the good points nor trying to correct the bad. All the main work should have been done beforehand.

✘　DONT, if you can help it, encroach on other competitor's space when warming up.

✘　DONT gallop near other competitors. You may indeed have a lazy horse who benefits from it just before a test, but find somewhere out of the way to do it, where it won't upset all the other horses.

✘　DON'T forget that your turnout is as important as that of your horse and shows your dedication to the task in hand, as well as respect for the judge. A shabby turnout on the part of rider or horse is often matched by a nondescript performance.

✘　DON'T blame the horse for a less than perfect test. Ninety-nine times out of 100 it is the rider who could have done better.

Leaping Ahead – Cross Country Riding

To have begun is half the job:
be bold and be sensible.

Horace (Quintus Horatius Flaccus) 65-8 BC

Riding across country needs special courage from both horse and rider. Fixed fences can be pretty formidable from any angle and tackling them at speed takes extra guts. The best way to start might be pleasure rides across country, though hunting and drag hunting offers the best base for fast riding while keeping your wits about you.

Obviously, you need to be a good rider with a safe, independent seat before even thinking about jumping cross country and you would want to start off in a small way with low jumps and no pressure involved regarding speed. If you aim to compete, an expert trainer is essential.

Pleasure rides

Sponsored and pleasure rides are becoming very popular and will give you an opportunity, like hunting, to ride over private land, which would not normally be possible. With this in view, it is important to respect directional markers and to be careful when riding through stock or around crops. Do not attempt to do a short cut, or go home without telling an official, because if you fail to pass a steward it will be reported and a search party sent out.

Obviously your horse should be fit enough to do the shortest distance on the ride; but the beauty of these pleasure rides is that you can go at whatever pace you like and jump or not, as the fancy takes you.

If you are approaching a rider or group from behind, be very careful and only over-take once you have spoken to them. Pleasure rides are an

Even when in the company of a safe older horse, a youngster can easily become unnerved

ideal introduction for young horses who need to learn about travelling to a strange place and then to behave quietly in company which is why many people these days use pleasure rides to educate their young horses. A green horse, even when in the company of a safe 'nanny,' will be unnerved by a gang of other horses galloping by.

When jumping, etiquette and safety go hand in hand. Try not to get to close to the horse in front and if you are having a problem and your horse is stopping, or you need more time and space in order to introduce your horse to something new, let others go first rather than holding them up.

Horse Trials and Hunter Trials

Eventing, or horse trials, is the ultimate test of horse and rider, requiring courage, skill, discipline and fitness from both. The highest level is the three day event. A dressage test is followed by a speed and endurance day, with roads and tracks, steeplechase and cross-country phases covered in a certain time. This is followed by show jumping on the final day.

A one day event has the horse presented for a dressage, cross country and show jumping test all in one day and so you need plenty of experience in all three disciplines. The courses are shorter than in two and three-day horse trials and there are no roads and tracks nor steeple-chase phases.

British Eventing (BE) is the governing body regarding horse trials and all horses and riders have to be registered members of BE before being eligible to enter BE run events. The rule book is updated annually, so be sure to study a current copy before entering.

If competition day arrives and your horse does not look his usual chirpy self or has any physical discomfort, don't even consider competing in Horse Trials. It would not be fair to either of you and it is better to be safe than sorry. You owe him that.

On reaching the competition site make sure you don't block anyone when you park your box. Some have side as well as back ramps so look carefully before stopping. If you need to borrow anything, be certain to return it as soon as possible and if you find any lost equipment, take it to the secretary's tent.

If you have not been able to walk the course the day before and assuming all is well on your arrival, the first priority is to walk the course at least once and not more than four times (depending on the type of competition and the amount of time available). Comfortable footwear is a 'must' and wellies may be needed if there is a river to cross, or a water jump or if it is a wet day. Remember to keep the red flag on your right and the white on your left at all times. As there may already be early competitors on the course, be very careful when studying or climbing over fences that there is not a horse approaching; and always stand *well back* when you hear a steward's whistle blow. It is very difficult to concentrate if you have to take a dog with you on the course walk, especially as he must be on a lead, so you are really better to leave him in the lorry or at home. Remember that you are not allowed to walk the course on horseback. So it is up to you to have studied the appropriate approaches, take-offs and get-aways and to position your horse correctly at every fence. After all, he did not pace the strides required between the fences!

There are codes of behaviour to be followed at horse trials – even journalists are targeted. At Badminton members of the press are requested to be reasonably dressed AT ALL TIMES (the organisers capitals, not mine) and when working in the arena men are required to wear a jacket and tie.

Forbidden areas include the whole of the fenced area at Control HQ (start and finish) while the cross-country is in progress and the collecting ring during the dressage and show jumping phases.

If you have friends attending the trials as spectators do impress upon them not to cross the course unless it is absolutely safe to do so *and* to keep their dogs on leads and under control. Mobile telephones are most definitely not permitted in the main arena during the competition.

Hunter Trials take place in the spring and in the autumn and just involve riding around a cross country course. Sometimes they are judged on style with a time section, sometimes they are judged on faults and the round with no faults and closest to the optimum time wins.

The accepted code of dress for hunter trials used to be a tweed coat with hunting boots and hat, but nowadays many competitions make it a condition of entry that riders wear back protectors and since these do not fit comfortably under coats, cross country dress is becoming the - norm.

A stock (hunting tie), secured with a pin, should be worn for neck support and protection from the undergrowth (which can be decidedly scratchy)! Gloves must be of the non-slip variety: wearing leather gloves on leather reins is asking for trouble. You never know what the weather is going to do and wet gloves on wet reins are lethal.

At hunter trials, numbers may be collected from either the secretary's tent or the horsebox park. Hang on to them as often there is a deposit to make sure they are not lost. Don't hog the practice fence, stopping others from having their turn. Two or three jumps should be quite sufficient.

If you have a problem while on the course, always make way for a following competitor before trying again. It is not really good manners to take a 'lead' from the competitor who has passed you after a refusal.

If you have more than three stops at a fence you will be eliminated and must leave the course *at a walk.* (At some informal, unaffiliated competitions you may, after asking the fence judge go on to the next fence). In any case,do not argue with the fence judge as to how many refusals you had. It is his job to count. However, sometimes clerical mistakes are made and if you discover, for example, that you have been given a stop and you actually jumped clear, you will find in the schedule or rules, the procedure for making a complaint, which you are entitled to do. You will find you will get further with it if you are tactful, rather than if you are belligerent !

If you get out of control on the course - it happens- or need to circle to regain control, be certain you are not in anyone's way. If galloping behind another rider you could shout, as politely as possible in the circumstances, to let them know you are coming.

Should a pedestrian be in your way on the course, shout 'stand still'. This way you know exactly where they are and will be able to manoeuvre around them. Shouting ' look out!' or 'get out of the way!' may result in them running for cover, but in which direction ? It will slow you up. Better for them to stand still !

After the event walk your horse quietly back to the box and have his saddle removed. The following day either take him out for a good walk (perhaps in hand) to stretch his legs, or turn him out to relax. In the stable when checking him over hand rubbing is always appreciated by a sensitive horse.

Drag Hunting

Some people think that drag hunting is so tied up with tradition and correct etiquette that it is difficult for a newcomer to learn the 'ins' and 'outs'. But nothing could be further from the truth. Behaviour on the hunting field is nothing more than common sense and obvious courtesy. In time the new comer will begin to understand the terms used.

When hunting for the first time, it is important to telephone the secretary first, to find out when it is best to visit. You will also be able to find out cost, where the 'meet' is and where it will be best to park.

On arrival at the meet, park tidily, where you are not obstructing gateways or the exit route of another lorry. Once you are mounted, have your 'cap' (either a cheque or cash) ready to give to the secretary. He will be looking out for you, so don't worry about not being able to find him ! After your cap is paid, find out from the secretary who the 'field master' is (that is the person who will be organising the day and whom you will follow). If you are reasonably sure your horse will behave in close proximity to others, it is good manners to say 'Good morning' to the Master, but if not, introduce yourself as soon as possible after the meet. If you are worried that your horse may misbehave, it is prudent to attach a green ribbon to his tail and stay at the back until he has settled. The green ribbon tells other members of the field that your horse is inexperienced and they will give him room. By the same token, you must be careful not to 'crowd' a horse wearing a green ribbon. If you are coming up behind someone fast, for example in a narrow track, or a gateway, you might see them putting their hand in the small of their back, palm facing out. This is a polite way of indicating that their horse is worried about your impending arrival and might kick you.

A red ribbon on a horse's tail indicates that he is likely to kick. Although kickers are expected to stay at the rear of the field when hacking from place to place, when you are running, you might find yourself close to a kicker. So beware.

If the pack, or a single hound passes you, it is essential to have your horse facing towards it. It is the worst possible form to kick or ride over hounds.

When you are running, take care to follow the Master, as the line is already pre-ordained and he knows exactly where to jump safely. 'Larking' does not tend to occur with drag hunting because the field is kept busy galloping and jumping, for the duration of their ride, but it is worth mentioning. The term refers to jumping unnecessary fences when hounds are not running. It is not only bad form, but also a stupid practice. At the end of the day your horse may need every ounce of stamina to complete a fast run and you will be cursing yourself for having wasted his energy jumping to and fro over an unnecessary jump at lunch-time.

If you have the misfortune of smashing a fence and there is stock in the field, you must dismount and make it as stock proof as possible. If you are jumping from arable to arable or there is no stock, you do not have to do this, but in both instances, you must report the damage to the secretary.

If a message comes down the field such as 'gate please' (which means for the last one through to shut the gate), pass the message on and be sure before you do, that you are not the last !

Even if you only stay out for half the day, it is polite to thank the Master, and to say 'Good night" – even if it is only 2.00pm. A thank you note to the Master a few days later is a welcome gesture and will ensure a warm welcome the next time you wish to visit. So if you and your horse enjoy yourselves, the next step is to subscribe, so that you can hunt on a regular basis and are no longer a 'visitor'.

Courtesy Check List
Competitive cross country riding

✓ DO remember to prepare yourself mentally as well as physically before an event. Positive thinking is the key to success. Mind control is important and people find different ways of coping. Some need to be relaxed and others need to get worked up. Many have 'lucky' items as talismans.

✓ DO remember it is up to you to keep a record of the number of points your horse acquires in official horse trials.

✓ DO ask advice from an expert if you have reached a stumbling block in your training.

✓ DO remember that in the many cases the organisers do the job voluntarily, and even if you have had a disaster of a day, it costs nothing to go into the Secretary's tent and say 'thank you'.

✖ DON'T enter for competition until you and your horse are competent and fit.

✖ DON'T forget to study the rules carefully.

✖ DON'T forget to look out for fellow riders.

✖ DON'T hog practice fences.

✖ DON'T give up when things go wrong. Try again and again.

Courtesy Check List
Non- competitive cross country riding

✓ DO be aware of other riders and horses and give them room.

✓ DO follow the Master, or directional markers and stay within recommended boundaries.

✓ DO make yourself useful; the saying 'one good deed deserves another' often rings true and you may be very glad one day of having caught someone's horse.

✓ DO ride straight so that you don't balk other horse approaching a fence beside you.

✓ DO respect horses wearing red or green ribbons on their tails.

✓ DO tell the Secretary if you have noticed any damage.

✓ DO remember to shut gates behind you.

✖ DON'T follow too closely and 'get on the heels' of other horses when jumping.

✖ DON'T allow your horse to 'run' along a fence line, if he has stopped; you might cause an accident if another horse is approaching at speed.

✖ DON'T have your horse in a position where he might kick hounds.

✖ DON'T get in the way of hunt servants.

✖ DON'T barge or push in gateways.

✖ DON'T, if you happen to venture on the public highway hold up traffic. Get up onto the verge or find a gateway to stand in.

Over the Top – Show Jumping

*Half the failures in life arise from pulling in
one's horse as he is leaping.*

Augustus Hare (1792 – 1834)

Show jumping is possibly the most enjoyable equestrian sport to watch on television and, as many people seem to spend a great deal of time in front of the 'box', this could well account for its tremendous popularity. It was one of the first sports to become a TV favourite in the early 1950s and achieved its zenith in the early 70s when it captivated audiences of over 11 million.

Most riders with an adventurous spirit want to jump at some stage. Unless they have had bad experiences in the past most horses enjoy jumping. I think they like jumping across country better than the confined and more restricted jumps in the ring, but with good and sympathetic training they do come to view it with as much enthusiasm as their riders.

Perhaps one of the most attractive facets of show jumping competitions is that the basic rules are so simple compared to other disciplines. It is easy to see the clock in the corner with the time ticking on and whether a pole is knocked down or not!

In the early days of show jumping, style was everything and no faults were given for refusals. After three, however, it was thought the crowd might become bored so rider and horse were asked politely to try another fence! The sport was first included in the Olympics in 1912 when, like most things, it was for men only. It was not until 1956 that Pat Smythe became the first lady to ride at this prestigious event.

If you are considering show jumping in a serious manner it will be necessary to join British Show Jumping Association, (BSJA). This is the governing body of the sport in Great Britain. The BSJA rules book is a mine of information and contains pages on conduct and discipline which should be carefully studied.

It is pointed out that no one is allowed to argue with a judge or show official at a show and that abusive or threatening language, incivility or contempt towards them is not allowed. It seems so sad that statements like this should have to be made and appear in print. There are twenty points in all and they should be well noted for trouble free competing.

There are many traps to beware of, like starting your round before the bell has sounded for the start, or taking the jumps in the wrong order, particularly important to get right when team jumping. But, I think perhaps the greatest mistake to avoid is buying a horse either beyond or below your own capabilities.

David Broome remained at the top of his career for over 25 years and his philosophy on show jumping was this: 'While a good rider can get the best out of a horse and make it jump as high as it can, not even a good rider can make a horse jump higher than it is capable of doing'.

It is not always realised that a condition of registration is that all horses and ponies are also registered with the British Horse Database and that this is a lifetime registration. Most would agree with experienced show jumper Graham Fletcher that the horse's ability to jump would seem to come before its breeding. He quotes a late Chinese leader, Deng Xiaoping who said, 'It doesn't matter whether the cat is white or black, as long as it catches mice'.

Not every owner will ever find out about the breeding of their horse or pony and they just have to go on the database as unknown breeding. But there is a way, according to Graham, to get good horses for whom the owners do not have any written documentation, onto the database. Apparently, the Anglo-European Studbook will provide registration papers if blood samples from the horse and its dam are approved, and if suitable documentation about the stallion can be produced. This would seem an excellent solution for a good horse and well worth the expense involved.

Courtesy Check List

✓ DO remember that intelligent equestrian reading and guidance from the ground are essential for success in any of the horsy disciplines.

Do keep your wits about you in the collecting ring…

✓   DO remember that walking the course is not the right time for social chat.

✓   DO keep your wits about you in the collecting ring.

✓   DO make sure that your practice fence, if you have been jumping a high or unusual one, is put back down to a reasonable height for others to warm up over when you are finished.

✓   DO ask a member of the ground crew to re-adjust a pole dislodged from the last round before the bell goes for you to start your round.

✓ DO remember that unauthorised assistance during a round is unacceptable but that does not include bringing back a loose horse after a fall, helping a rider to re-adjust saddlery or to remount.

✓ DO, if you decide to retire, come back to a walk or halt, salute (as for dressage) or nod politely at the judge and walk from the arena.

✖ DON'T forget to keep the red flag on the practice fence to your right and the white flag to your left.

✖ DON'T cut any one up in your approach to the practice fence.

✖ DON'T hog the practice fence.

✖ DON'T gallop out of the ring after you have finished your round.

Show Business

Always to be the best, and to be distinguished above the rest.

Homer.

Involving yourself in showing is similar to being on the stage in a theatrical production. You will have spent many hours of rehearsal and preparation and probably experience a lot of butterflies in the stomach. The quote from Homer sums it up well – the desire to win and know that you and your horse or horses are simply the best in that discipline.

It goes almost without saying that there are a great many right and wrong ways to do things and that the more you know, the better you will do. Apart from your side of things, the planning, practice, memorising the procedure and location; for this presentation there is the horse to be briefed as well.

Before you even consider the possibility of entering this minefield of 'doing the right thing' it is important to realise that showing is subjective and the results are in the eyes of the judge. If a particular judge keeps marking you down for some reason you do not understand, go to a different show. Another judge may consider you a winning combination. You may believe your horse is the best in the world but, unfortunately, a judge may not be of the same opinion. If you cannot accept this premise and the fact that you may not even be placed, then showing is not for you!

An example of this would be that there are some judges who do not like chestnut horses. Therefore it is not sensible to take your chestnut to a show where that particular judge is on that day. It would be the epitome of bad manners to argue and it would never be forgotten. The best approach is to work hard, choose your judges carefully and look forward to the next one, keeping your fingers crossed for better luck.

Preparation

The showing season lasts approximately seven months, from March until October, so you need to be prepared well in advance. If you have any queries about the classes then do telephone beforehand. Do not turn up on the day expecting everything to be okay. You may have misunderstood part of a schedule. In order to be completely organised it is important to read the schedule well beforehand and check the small print. Remember that show secretaries work hard often for no reward at all, so it is not fair to burden them with queries and telephone calls at the last minute which could have been avoided by careful reading.

 Although some people do show horses in different categories it is still not correct to do so. Schedules must be read carefully. Some will state that horses can be entered in one category but not another.

Do not expect individual attention from busy organisers. Always be polite to them no matter how nervous or panic-stricken you may be.

Thanking both show organisers and sponsors should go without saying. If you belong to a riding club, make an effort to help in a voluntary capacity at some stage, at least once a season.

Some basic pointers

It is not really correct to use a numnah when showing so if your horse is cold backed you will have to be inventive. Choose one that matches the saddle and is not intrusive, or have a piece of sheepskin cut to fit the saddle. (While on the subject of correct tack, do remember that not wearing a double bridle could lose your horse the championship).

Some people believe whiskers should always be left on the horse's face for the purpose of acting as feelers, but this does not look correct when showing. Similarly, a full tail plaited is not as eye-catching as one that has been correctly pulled. Plaited manes should always be stitched, certainly no rubber bands or white tape.

If you must wear a buttonhole make sure it is discreet. White breeches are inappropriate and gloves (always brown leather) must be worn. A cane, which should be malacca or leather covered, must be carried to complete the picture.

If you feel you need another kind of whip in order to strike your horse, perhaps you should not have entered this or, indeed, any other class.

Hats with chin straps are *de rigeur*, and if there are no ring stewards it is quite in order for a spectator or groom to give a 'leg up'.

Be sure you know how to trot a horse up well and never argue with a vet or a judge. It has been said that 'anyone can ride in the show ring, but to show in the ring is an art'. Start at small shows and learn carefully as you go along. You will have spent much time ensuring your horse or pony looks smart so, whether riding or showing in hand, make sure you look equally as smart.

Tweed jackets are correct for hunter, cob and riding horse classes while ladies should wear black or navy for showing hacks. If in doubt, dress down and stick with a tweed jacket rather than navy or black. Leather gloves are a must, but always keep a pair of string gloves handy in case of rain. Wet leather gloves on wet leather reins are useless. Ear-rings and other jewellery should not be worn, nor should gold and silver striped nail varnish!

It is correct for riders, but not judges, to wear spurs in showing classes. Do practise at home or you may find you have too much forward impulsion

Side-saddle

A word about side-saddle riders. If you wish to enter a competition such as working hunter which is usually judged astride, you will have to ask the judge's permission to ride side-saddle and have an ordinary saddle at his disposal.

In actual side-saddle classes it is the rider who is looked at critically. Clothes are very important. Good second-hand ones can be a better fit and give a more classy appearance than some new. The right toe must never show, nor must breeches be seen beneath the habit which should be navy or black. The bowler should sit straight on your head and a veil and bun complete the picture.

On a lighter note; I once knew a gentleman who was very keen on riding side-saddle and, in fact, rode very elegantly but whether he ever rode competitively and what he wore, I cannot imagine !

Help from the Ground

The groom's help is invaluable and he or she also has rules of etiquette to follow. Sadly, over the years informality seems to be creeping into the show ring but some acceptable tenets still stand.

A groom will not be allowed into the ring if not wearing a hat, hacking jacket and shirt and tie. One groom recounts the story of being at Windsor in the ring on a day which started off by being chilly but which later became hot. She was wearing a Puffa jacket and as the heat increased she took out the sleeves to change it into a waistcoat. To her dismay she was sent out of the ring and now would not consider wearing any other kind of coat than a hacking jacket.

At the Show ground

Always arrive early. There is nothing worse than arriving somewhere fraught and anxious because your nervous state will be transmitted to the horse and things may go from bad to worse. A calm and efficient start will make all the difference. It is rude to enter a class after judging has begun and the judge is within his or her rights to refuse to judge that person.

Take care that standards of good practice do not drop outside the show ring. Both the lorry park and practice ring are places to show your consideration to others. Always walk back to your box: trotting or cantering

Asking for trouble

back is simply not on. Skimming past much too close to other horses is asking for trouble from both horses and riders; likewise squeezing through narrow gaps.

When parking your box remember to give others plenty of room. Some owners like to tie their horses up outside, so give them space to manoeuvre and don't have horses tied up to boxes back to back!

It is also bad to leave them unattended or tied up for too long. If there is to be a long wait, put the animal in the box where he can rest in peace.

Hay nets tied to the back of boxes will absorb the surrounding petrol fumes, especially when travelling on busy roads. If you must tie them up at the show take care they are tied short enough so that the horses do not get their heads or feet caught up in them and panic.

When riding in a practice arena give consideration to others and to your horse. Do not wear him out before he even gets in to the ring and do not hog all the space. Others want to practise too. If you are riding in a team do not criticise another member you think is not performing well. It is essential to be supportive all the time.

In the Ring

It is customary to enter the ring on the right rein and whatever happens do not stand away from the others to make yourself seen: walking inside the rest of the class or inside another competitor obscuring the judge's view will not go in your favour.

Remember to show the judge your number and keep to the protocol of that particular arena with regard to passing left to left, etc. (So far as I am aware, it is only members of the Spanish Riding School who pass right to right).

Ride a wide corner to keep out of a bunch and keep alert so you are always in the right place at the right time. But do not keep your eyes fixed on the judge while you are riding.

Do not ride too close to the horse in front. Choose your moment so you have plenty of room. Even if your nerves are stretched to breaking point by the unusual behaviour of your horse or any other circumstance, never hit your animal because you have lost your temper. When you get home think carefully about what happened and consider what you could have done in order to prevent the situation or alleviate it in some way.

Nerves are a dreadful nuisance but most of us suffer from them. Spare a thought for the rider competing on another's mount. The pressure can be great with the owner's expectations sometimes exceeding the possibilities. A non-horsy owner's criticisms could be very hard to take, especially one continually expecting the rider to do better and dictating the conditions of riding, like the length of stirrup leather, shortness of the reins and so on.

Do not ever try any unsporting tricks like covering up a rival. It would make the judge extremely irritated (not to mention the rival!).

Keep your eyes on the steward and when called in to line nod to him and walk on. If you are short and your horse is tall stewards can be invaluable in giving a leg up.

You may talk quietly to your companions, but not when the judge is coming round, and do not offer unsolicited information about your horse; it will not be welcome.

If asked to give an individual show, do not get carried away: produce something to show that your horse is responsive and obedient for not more than a minute and a half. When asked to gallop in the show ring, do not just 'go for it'. Be sure you are balanced going into the corner and lengthen your stride out of it, being sure to bring him back before the next one.

When you are trotting your animal up for the judge make sure that he slows down soon enough and does not collide with the one in front, causing a concertina action down the line.

When you know the judge will have to ride your horse try not use a small saddle. If the judge is large he will not be comfortable, so (as long as the saddle still fits the horse) being kind by using a larger saddle may help you in the long run. The same applies to stirrup leathers and irons. It would be kind to alter the length of the irons in readiness for the judge to ride. They might not be exactly right but he or she would appreciate the thought. If you are down the line, you can always check the length using your cane as a measure, from the saddle of a horse who has already been ridden.

Incidentally, if the judge does ride your horse, do have the grace to watch and see how the animal behaves. He should go well and it is extremely discourteous to chat to a neighbour while he is giving his show. You could learn something to your advantage and, after all, it is for your benefit.

A word of warning! As the judge is mounting your horse, do not

Not helping your cause

launch into the animal's life history. The judge does not want to know. Also, remember that not only is he or she judging the horse, but the way in which it is presented as well, and for goodness' sake smile. If you look gloomy the judge will think there is something wrong with one or both of you!

When considering the attitude of a judge or judges do be reasonable. They have probably travelled some distance to be there and they are only human. Jane Phillipps, who has been judging hunters, hacks, cobs, side-saddle and riding horses since 1979 says that the norm at the Dublin Show is to judge about 14 horses in a day, whereas at the Cheshire Show one year she judged 70 through the day. Now that requires some stamina!

Perhaps the most important thing to remember about showing is never to question the judge's decision. Never consider yourself above criticism and be your own most severe critic. That way you will improve your chances of nearing the top. No matter how wrong you consider the outcome, remember that judging is all a matter of opinion – the judge's!

If you should be lucky enough to gain a prize, even though it is not the one you coveted, smile and thank the judge. A gentleman should take off his hat. As you gallop round the ring, take care not to overtake. Keep politely behind the horse who has beaten you and congratulate the winner.

When your horse has finished his class take him back to rest. Do not spend the rest of the show sitting on his back watching the others. It is not fair to him and he will only get tired and irritated.

If your horse has done well, or is tired, and you decide not to enter the classes originally intended do remember to tell the stewards you are giving your horse a break and save them the irritation of waiting and calling you on the Tannoy when you have changed your mind.

Pointers for Child Riders and Adult Handlers

Manners are a very important part of any pony's training. While things such as standing still while being mounted will have been taught at home, there are other matters which make life much easier which he will only learn by experience.

There are rules such as standing in a crowd of strangers in the collecting ring without your pony kicking or biting other ponies or people, standing still while hoof oil is being applied, or girths tightened, or waiting his turn at the practice jump without getting over excited and so on. A good rule of thumb would be not to put a small child on a pony that is less than steady when it gets to a show. For the large number of happy polished turnouts one sees at shows ,unfortunately there are still too many tearful, tense and unsafe combinations, hence friction which does not make for a pleasant day for stewards or judges.

Even adults are culprits and may be seen standing about getting cold then expecting a horse or pony to perform well. Keep him moving. If you leave young children alone before a class they will probably stand about chatting to friends, so see that the young rider exercises in a quiet place beforehand and then leave him or her to get on with it. Do not hang over the rails making signs and shouting last minute instructions. You will only confuse and upset both pony and child.

When showing in hand, walk and trot by the horse's shoulder. Do not drag the animal along. Run in step, trying to move well yourself. Grooms must be neatly dressed. Leading rein handlers can wear outfits to match the pony but must be able to run comfortably in them. Ponies with white socks can be ridden-in with their bandages on, which can then be removed at the last minute.

It is perfectly legitimate to describe a pony as 'Welsh' without having any papers. However, if he is not legally registered he cannot be shown in classes for registered ponies.

Welsh cobs, colts and stallions particularly, used to be taught to stand with their hind legs stretched out behind them but today this is not considered essential.

Once in the ring, do not let anyone fidget about with the pony since this will distract both him and his rider. Be wary of providing tit-bits. You could come unstuck on the day you forget to put them in your pocket! Teach the riders to enter competitions for the pleasure of taking part and be humble about not winning, making sure it always remains fun!

Judging

As the person in authority, who will be weighing up the pros and cons of different animals and their riders it is up to you to set as good an example of etiquette in the ring as you can. Owners, riders and handlers will be looking to you for fair judgement after taking everything into consideration

If invited to judge it is essential to confirm the date and time, and which classes are to be judged, in order to prevent any unfortunate misunderstandings. Make sure you have the necessary passes sent to you in good time. Do not accept the reassurance that if you tell them on the gate who you are 'they' will let you in. Take it from one who knows, it is more likely that 'they' will do no such thing. Their instructions are only to admit entrants with money or a pass. Only embarrassment will follow as a long queue forms while you are trying to convince the gate keepers that you are who you say you are.

Like the competitors, get there early. Allow for heavy traffic, accidents, hold-ups, complicated journeys, getting lost and queues to get in. There are not many occasions when people are welcomed with open arms for breakfast, but this is definitely one of them.

Getting there early will also mean that you can have a look at your ring, and especially the going.

Remember that you will be under scrutiny all day and that the competitors will be sitting in judgement on your behaviour in the ring. You are as much on stage as they are. It would seem unforgivable for a judge to stand chatting to a steward with his or her back to an unfortunate competitor who has already been deemed of insufficiently high standard for further scrutiny. Yet I have seen this happen. Being ignored is always offensive and particularly in a showing situation. At unaffiliated shows, the showing classes are often well supported and the competitors pay their entry fee for their horses to be judged. If it is a class in which the judge would normally ride the horses, it is the height of discourtesy for him or her not to 'try' every horse. Even if Mr. Very Ancient Bored and Plain, standing at the end of a line of twenty horses, *looks* unlikely to come up the line on his ride, he might just surprise you and delight his rider.

If a horse is patently unsound or unsafe, and you really don't want to ride him, you must be tact personified. Your diplomatic skills will be tested, but it is likely, if the subject is approached in the right way, that the rider will agree.

Once, when judging, I made my choice for all the right reasons and was pleased with the decision. It was afterwards, when one of the organisers approached me, that I realised how unpopular was that decision. Did I not realise that Baroness So-and-So ALWAYS came first and what could they say to her now? This anecdote brings back the subjectivity of the discipline. While you may be lucky enough to become first several times, you will not remain top of the list forever.

A judge can only give an opinion on what is on view on the day. An offending horse probably wore a halo last week, but if he is misbehaving now, that is beside the point.

Courtesy Check List

✓   DO keep an open mind on your horse's potential.

✓   DO study the schedule and choose your class or classes with care.

✓   DO arrive in plenty of time.

✓   DO be courteous to stewards at all times – and, in fact, to everyone else.

✓ DO give the judge a pleasant smile.

✖ DON'T wear clothes which will stand out in a crowd.

✖ DON'T wear jewellery.

✖ DON'T push in front of others when in the ring, or anywhere else.

✖ DON'T argue with the judge's decision.

✖ DON'T go to a show without practising at home.

A Word about Ponies and 'Pony Club'

Education has for its object the formation of character
Social statics (1850)

Joining the Pony Club is the best introduction a young person can have for horsemanship in the future. Pony Club rallies and camps are wonderful training grounds. At camp, in particular, instructors have the time to teach young children how to behave around ponies and other children with ponies, as well as to ride.

Obviously, the main aims of camp (apart from the children having enormous fun with their ponies) is for them to receive fairly concentrated instruction over several days, to help improve their riding and stable management skills. It is here that they will also become aware of other requirements of tidiness and 'sporting' behaviour. Here they learn that it is necessary during competitions to keep your coat buttoned up, for girls to wear a hair net, to be generally neat and tidy and the reasons why. They learn that it is not acceptable to be cheeky, or indulge in a tantrum. Boys learn when to take off their hats in politeness. Children learn how to work as a team in the yards and what is expected of team members in competition too.

Keeping up standards at all times means adhering to a correct code of dress. Learning to tie a stock or tie properly is important and so is the fact that it is wrong to use a dandy brush on a pony's mane and tail. You want to keep it, not brush it out!

The need for correct dress does not mean that it is necessary to spend a fortune on clothes. They should be serviceable and safe, but it should be emphasised that shoes are not correct footwear, especially trainers. A foot that slips out of the stirrup can be as dangerous as a foot that does not easily become dislodged if the rider is thrown and the foot stays in the stirrup. Being dragged along the ground by a bolting pony is nobody's idea of fun. Most Pony Clubs keep a selection of second- hand clothes and tack which parents often sell or give to the club to help raise funds. Really good items can be bought in this way for a fraction of the cost of new gear.

The sooner a child learns the basics of riding the better, and he or she will get a thorough grounding through their involvement with Pony Club. Knowing that the red flag is always on the right when jumping will stand the child in good stead later on. Knowing that it is unforgivable to beat a pony in front of an obstacle and that bad riding ruins the most willing of ponies should be instilled from the start. Similarly, that jerking a pony in the mouth is guaranteed to make him stop and that he will refuse in future. Children absorb all this important information painlessly.

Pony club parents

It is natural for every parent to want the best for their child and to see the child achieve great things. There is a tendency however, (unless nipped in the bud very quickly), for mothers to do all the work instead of the child. A good DC (District Commissioner) will soon put this right, tactfully explaining that the child will never learn, for example, to put on a bridle, if mum does it all the time.

When the child is being taught, it is good manners to observe quietly in the background. Many children settle much quicker, are able to take fresh ideas or methods 'on board' and concentrate better when their parents play a passive role. There is nothing worse for an instructor than to be teaching a jumping lesson, and to have little Jimmy's dad roaring conflicting instructions from the side-lines.

Sadly, it is the case that some parents are less than well behaved at rallies, complaining bitterly that their child should have been put in the same ride as someone else. This sets a bad example to the off-spring. Putting together rides is done with great thought and care, and there is generally a very good reason why child A has not been put in the same group as child B. If there is something with which you do not agree, take it up with the DC – in private.

In any club there is always an enthusiastic core who end up doing all the work. In the context of Pony Clubs, it really is a great help to lend a hand once in a while . Those parents who are prepared to load and unload jumps, help put up tents and set up arenas are always appreciated, as are those who will cook and wash up at camp.

Finally, Pony Club is not a cheap baby sitting service; not only is it discourteous, but it is not a very bright idea to leave your child and pony in camp, then take off abroad on a second honeymoon for the week.

Pony Club Instructors

If you enjoy teaching children and coping with their hairy four legged friends, nothing can be quite as rewarding as teaching for the Pony Club. In a single 'ride' (that is group) you may get a variety of interesting challenges, from a brave little person on a truly unco-operative pony to a nervous child on a valuable competition pony.

When you are invited to teach at a rally, you will need to find out the standard of the ride, and the facilities you will be able to use. If you really enjoy taking, for example the the lead-rein ride, or the 12 year old 'flyers' or ones working for 'B' test, say so. Also discuss remuneration. Pony Club is a voluntary youth organisation, but most clubs these days accept the fact that an instructor can not afford to give up the whole day without some form of payment. However, remuneration may not be what you are used to, and if you are unhappy with the offer, it is much better to know in advance and to negotiate rather than find out on the day and cause any embarrassment.

However well or poorly a pony behaves, however flashy or plain he may be, you will usually find that he is 'one of the family' and often deeply cherished. So a great deal of tact is needed on the part of instructors when making suggestions regarding that pony (especially if it is being beastly)!

If you find an article of tack fitting in an unusual way or perhaps rather more tightly than normal, always ask the child first if there is a reason for it, before altering it. This is both for safety and courtesy reasons. Mum, standing on the side-lines in her wellies, may well have cleaned the bridle and put it back two holes short. On the other hand, she might be an ex-Olympic champion, who knows exactly what she is doing and has put the snaffle a bit higher than technically correct, because 'Furry Fred' has a tendency to get his tongue over the bit, which makes it difficult for his rider to steer or stop and is a nuisance for every-one.

If a saddle is really putting a child into an impossible position, you will need to speak to the parents about it, as well as the child, but tactfully.

They may not have realised especially if the saddle came with the pony. Parents are unlikely to change anything unless an informed explanation can convince them a change would be for the better.

Never make drastic alterations to bitting arrangements. A pony wearing a severe bit may go sweetly on the flat for an hour and make you feel that he should be in a snaffle, until he sees the first fence of the day... .

As an instructor, you lead by example, in your behaviour and your dress. Punctuality is important. It is better to arrive before the children, so that you can set up your exercises and have your teaching area ready for action. If you are teaching dismounted, be dressed ready to ride – unless you are taking the under 10s. It is not only unprofessional in the extreme, but also discourteous to your host and a bad example to the children to turn up in filthy breeches, trainers or dirty boots and without a hat of at least the safety standard which the children are required to wear. You may well need to ride a naughty horse or pony for a child, and for that you will need to be dressed appropriately.

If you are going to instruct mounted, be very sure that your horse is suitable for the task. He must be able to illustrate what you are teaching and contribute to the children's progress; if he is quiet enough for them to sit on, to learn the rudiments of, for example, shoulder-in, all the better. He must be mannerly. If young Suzie's saddle has slipped forwards and you need to help her adjust it, it is no good having a horse who won't stand by the pony without biting or kicking it and then won't let you mount again, because a pony from the ride next door has just galloped past. Your attention must be on the safety and enjoyment of your ride and the last thing you want is to be seated on something unreliable or green who will take your attention away from the children in your care.

In Pony Club, children learn to tackle their problems and find solutions. It is up to the instructor to be up-beat, never negative in suggestions, advice and instruction. Remember, the children are riding for fun.

Ponies

It can be a problem when a pony who is quiet and amiable with others it knows, (in effect members of its own herd) becomes excited and misbehaves in strange company. Also, two ponies who won't be separated from each other are a nuisance. But it should not let this put your child off joining Pony Club activities. It is here that he or she will learn how to manage and improve the pony's behaviour. If the pony is likely to kick, tie a broad red tape in a bow on his tail. On your arrival at the rally go straight to the organiser and inform him or her of the problem, whatever it might be. The instructor will be notified, and your child and pony will be given especial help in overcoming the problem.

Pony club takes the safety of the children at rallies extremely seriously, which is why stallions are not allowed to attend, *unless* the District Commissioner gives specific permission in advance.

Courtesy Check List

✓ DO allow the children to do the work and the instructors to do the teaching at rallies.

✓ DO offer your help in the background if you intend to remain on site for the rally.

✓ DO remember that children are impressionable and will look to adults as role models.

✓ DO be positive and patient. Children come to Pony Club to learn. If a child arrives for the first time and fault is found in everything, this can be deeply discouraging and upsetting.

✖ DONT arrive to instruct without being ready and dressed to ride.

✖ DONT try to instruct from the back of a green or unsuitable horse.

✖ DONT regard Pony Club camp and rallies as a cheap baby sitting option.

✖ DONT leave before your child has said thank-you to his or her instructor, to the organiser and if possible, the land owner.

✖ DONT cause a situation, (whether teaching, organising or attending as a parent), whereby the safety and fun of the children is compromised.

In the Driving Seat

A place for everything and everything in its place.
Mrs Beeton (1836–65)

Never was there a saying more appropriate to driving. Although appearing in the Book *of Household Management* (1861) and written by an Englishwoman on the domestic arts, the sentiment applies perfectly to carriage driving, where it is vital to follow a routine procedure when harnessing up and putting to. The same sequence should be followed faithfully each time so that mistakes are less likely to be made and the horse is confident with the consistency. A final check should always be made before mounting. Three cheers for Mrs Beeton!

This sport which is fast growing on both sides of the Atlantic has much to recommend it. Friends and family can enjoy equitation together, and a much-loved riding horse or pony can sometimes be trained successfully to go in harness, giving the best of both worlds. All you need is a well trained animal safely harnessed to a sound, roadworthy vehicle and a competent driver.

So, in spite of increasing congestion on the roads, carriage driving is a sport on the up, and not only in Great Britain.

The Carriage Association of America and the American Driving Society have large memberships and driving is increasing in Europe and Australia. There are clubs and societies and the membership of all of these has grown dramatically in the last thirty-five years. The British Driving Society (BDS) currently has over 5,000 members. Like all good executive secretaries, Mrs Jenny Dillon of the BDS has her finger on the pulse of carriage driving in this country and can supply names, addresses and relevant information. Before the 1950s carriage driving was such an integral part of life that there were few clubs. Now over 200 shows are affiliated to the BDS every year and there are many more unaffiliated. The world's largest one day driving show is held at Smith's Lawn, Windsor, in June each year.

Carriages are reminiscent of Jane Austen novels, and if certain rules are followed, they are eye-catching and elegant.

It seems that most horsy people are interested in 'having a go' at some stage in their lives. Legend has it that as much care should be taken of a carriage as a gentleman would formerly take of his wardrobe.

Requirements for Driving

The necessary requisites are well-mannered, fit horses, a well built carriage, good harness and an abundance of sound horsemastership. When choosing the horse consider the work to be done. A flashy type, (horse, not person!) may look good in the show ring but be most unsuitable for wandering round country lanes. It is also difficult to match animals of unusual appearance if a pair is needed, but native ponies usually breed true to type so you could find another to make a pair much more easily. There are no firm rules, but a narrow fronted type is to be avoided as it would not be strong enough for the task.

Size is a matter of choice, though obviously a large animal will require more feeding and there could be difficulties in finding suitable tack. The disadvantage of choosing a small animal is that, when competing, he will be on equal terms against a larger one. Colour should not matter although, if you are showing, there will always be judges with personal preferences.

Show ponies are not usually suitable since, although they have their own stud book, they are a type and not a breed and are best suited to riding. Their legs are too fine and their temperaments are not usually suitable. Standardbreds have usually been driven only in lightweight racing sulkies and will need to be re-educated for private driving.

Individual breed societies will have official breed standards setting out the requirements in terms of conformation, characteristics and action. (The American Saddlebred has specialised and distinctive additional paces, including the slow rack or running walk and fast rack. Icelandic ponies have the tolt, a four-beat sequence). Donkeys should not be assumed to be stubborn or lazy. It is amazing what good basic training can do!

Local conditions will affect your decision. Hilly country will need a stronger type than that required to work only on the flat. Another consideration will be the number of people expected to go in the carriage, the weight of the vehicle and the height of the driver in relation to the carriage. Save yourself time and money by buying a horse or pony already trained to drive and with some experience behind him. When purchasing, ALWAYS take a vet to see the animal run up on hard ground and check for white marks, lumps and bumps. Take a note of his behaviour in traffic. Manners can be taught but some faults are more easily corrected than others. One thing the horse or pony must do is stand still when required.

Remember to avoid the dangerous vices, kicking, rearing, bolting and shying, like the plague!

When buying the vehicle, take advice from an expert to make sure it fits the horse and the driver, is perfectly balanced and suitable for the number of people wishing to take part in the sport. (For example, skeleton harness is only suitable for racing horses with a light sulky on a smooth, level track).

Basic Principles

As with all horse sports, the importance of sympathetic hands cannot be over stressed. Reins, which should always be brown, and suit the turnout, must not be too wide nor too narrow. Too wide will be cumbersome, too narrow will be difficult to hold in wet weather or if the horse is pulling. If too short, they could be snatched from the driver's hand if the horse stumbled, too long and they could be caught up in the driver's feet. (In America bearing reins are still standard on many types of harness but they are rarely fitted on English harness today). Always start driving with the reins in the left hand.

It should go without saying that the reins must never slap the horse's hindquarters, nor must the horse be struck on the hindquarters with the stock of a whip. This could encourage the horse to kick and/or break the whip. A driving whip should not be cracked like a hunting whip and it is not good practice to drive with the whip stuck in the whip socket on the vehicle, where it is of no practical use.

If you are going to be driving on the road you need a knowledge of speed. You want to know how fast you are travelling, as this will depend on the staying power of your horse. You must always keep an eye open for what is happening behind. There may be a faster carriage wishing to overtake.

Going up hill should be tackled at a trot, the pace increased slightly on approach. If the hill is long and steep, passengers should be asked to get out and walk, or stop and rest the horse/horses for a few minutes. Remember not to slow down when you reach the top of a hill. If you have others behind they will be stopped half way up! Clear signalling must be practised at all times.

When driving, remember reins, voice, whip, in that order. Also remember that passengers should never mount the vehicle until the driver is seated and in full control. The groom or assistant should stay by the horse's head until asked to move. This would seem to be commonsense, but it is surprising how many enthusiastic passengers are prepared to leap aboard the carriage without the driver! Never drive without an assistant and never leave a horse unattended while harnessed. If possible, wait until the horse is walking on before the assistant mounts, to keep the starting weight to a minimum. Similarly, on return, passengers must always dismount before the horse is taken from the vehicle and a horse should never be led out of the shafts. The carriage should be taken away

Passengers should never mount until the driver is seated and in full control

from him. An impatient horse could step forward too soon and be still partly attached.

The driver always sits on the offside. If he sat on the near side ,every movement of the right hand on the rein or whip would result in the passenger being nudged with his right elbow!

Traditionally, mounting was from the near side of a vanner ready to unload. You could be bowled over by oncoming traffic if you used the other side! Today, however, it is a matter of choice as to which side you prefer.

If the roads are slippery, studs will be needed in the shoes. If there is snow, pack the soles with grease. Always carry spares safely under the seat where they will not roll forward and never try to 'right' a vehicle in an accident before unharnessing the horses. A headcollar and lead rope should always be taken when going out.

Courtesy Check List
General Driving

✓   DO find the horse before the carriage.

✓   DO remember that time and patience are essential attributes when schooling a horse.

✓   DO bring the carriage to the horse. (An assistant should hold the horse while the driver brings the vehicle up from behind).

✓   DO make sure your animal is safe to be driven on the road before even turning out in traffic, for your own sake as well as that of other road users.

✓   DO endeavour to go out with a traffic-proof animal to give him confidence when he is learning.

✓   DO be sure to have public liability cover for both you and your horse. The British Driving Society has rules and regulations on lighting and driving on the road.

✓   DO remember that some insurance companies have been known not to pay up after an accident if there was not an accompanying person in the carriage, claiming it was irresponsible to drive without a second person.

✓   DO keep your knowledge of the Highway Code up to date;it changes.

✓   DO remember to go downhill at a walk.

✓   DO ask passengers to get out if the horse needs to rest for a while.

✓   DO remember that the majority of ridden horses view animals pulling carriages with pure horror if not used to seeing them. (My Russian mare's first sight of a donkey and cart trotting happily towards us caused her eyes to pop out on stalks while she turned round on a sixpence and bolted for home). So, if meeting a ridden horse, ask your groom to hold your animal's head while the rider sorts out their horse. If the horse and carriage stand still, it is some times possible to persuade the ridden horse to go past (possibly a little faster than requested!)

✓   DO keep your cool if you are driving and your horse bolts. You have several options. If the terrain is suitable, let him run while you concentrate on the steering. He may run out of steam and calm down or, perhaps you could direct him uphill. If all else fails, steer him towards some thing unjumpable.
Use your voice, but make sure it is not high pitched and squeaky with fear! If you talk to him, reassuring him all is well, it is likely that he will eventually listen and believe you.

✓   DO wear gloves. Unlined leather are best, but carry a spare pair in case the weather changes.

✖   DON''T let passengers get in the vehicle before the driver.

✖   DON''T use blinkers with decorative metal motifs attached with metal clips. Some folk can get carried away with the appearance of a piece of harness without realising the potential dangers.

✖   DON"T take a blinkered bridle from a horse while he is still put to a vehicle. Seeing the wheels coming from behind could make the horse bolt and cause a horrendous accident.

✖   DON"T use brown harness with a painted vehicle. (In times gone by, whether you had fittings of brass or white metal depended on the colour of the family's coat of arms).

✖   DON"T automatically assume that if a horse is misbehaving, he is naughty or wilfully disobedient. On the whole, horses want to please so causes need to be looked for. Discomfort could be caused by problems with tack , or injury to the mouth, limbs or feet.
However, if you are certain a horse is being deliberately unco-operative in refusing to do what you ask, he must be corrected there and then. Never think, 'I won't do that now', for whatever reason. The moment will be lost. Discipline must be enforced immediately WITHOUT losing your temper. Always use your voice before resorting to the whip. Your horse should know your different voice projections by now and will hopefully take notice.

✖   DON'T keep the whip permanently in its socket and the thong should not be whitened.

✖   DON'T decorate lamps with flowers or anything else.

✖   DON'T wear dazzling coloured clothes or any kind of fancy dress.

✖   DON'T wear trainers.

✖   DON'T use nylon whips for tandem driving as they cannot be folded in the traditional way.

Competing

Many people who take up carriage driving progress to a stage at which they become interested in the prospect of competing, either in driving trials or in the show ring.

Horse driving trials began in the early 1970s when new challenges were born. These trials are divided into phases and are based on the ridden three day event. The phases include presentation and dressage, the marathon, (an olympic feat of endurance across rough country and through water) and the final event, the cones.

Since driving trials demand a good deal of experience and expertise, not to mention expenditure, the majority of Whips gravitate, at least initially to the show ring. Of course, showing to a high standard also demands great expertise, but the novice has the opportunity to learn and progress up the scale. To this end, when choosing a first show, try to find a professionally run, low key one, both for your horse's sake and your own experience. Two basic points to remember are:

1. Before going to a show, make sure your horse has been out with another animal in harness or he may well be frightened. Remember that, though they may be side by side, they cannot see each other.

2. If you intend to compete, make sure your horse will have his feet picked up and inspected while put to a vehicle. The judge will not be amused if your horse suddenly becomes fractious!

Show Fever

I must go out to a show again
      I really don't know why.
And all I ask is a tandem cart
      And some reins to steer it by.
And the Wheeler kicks
      And it all goes wrong
With the sound of a shaft breaking
      And a broad grin
On the Leader's face
      And the Wheeler overtaking.

Bill Walrond (With apologies to John Masefield)

Courtesy Check List
Novice Whips at Shows

✓ DO tell the organiser of a rally if it is your first outing.

✓ DO see if you could follow an experienced Whip.

✓ DO remember that good manners are essential in showing classes. A judge will not be impressed by any one talking loudly, smoking or slouching and will not enjoy a worried expression. He or she will think something awful is about to happen any minute! Try to look pleasant and if possible, smile.

✖ DON'T trot around the ring overtaking everybody in sight, especially on the inside. This is most ill mannered and will be penalised. If the carriage in front is holding you up, take your animal away to make more room.

✖ DON'T forget that while your horse is allowed to extend in front of the judge, it is definitely *infra dig* to break gait into canter.

✖ DON'T stuff all your spares into a plastic carrier bag at the last minute. The judge may wish to inspect your boot which should be in good condition with spares neatly stored.

Advice from the Experts

Judging driving dressage competitions must be a nerve-racking business. HRH The Duke of Edinburgh KG KT is patron of the British Driving Society and in his book, *'Driving and Judging Dressage'* he discusses the problems facing those judges where a team of horses is expected to perform the same movements as one horse under saddle. He writes of the difficulty in getting four horses close to the markers or boards and discusses the perspectives of judges from different vantage points while stressing the importance of judges and competitors having the same target for the exercise!

This is a fascinating book for anyone interested in competition carriage driving. One of the author's pertinent comments regards presentation when he says that, though it may sound obvious, drivers and grooms always look better when they sit up straight and are appropriately and neatly dressed. The FEI has produced a booklet on the subject of dress but, in principle, it is the type of carriage and harness in use that decides the right dress.

Hard hats are worn for cross-country competition and are also sensible for daily driving. In the show ring gentlemen need a bowler or on more casual occasions, a cloth cap could be used. Smart occasions demand a suit. Ladies are advised to wear well fitting small brimmed hats in the show ring with coats, skirts and blouses which tone in colour. At cross-country events and driving meets, trousers are considered acceptable for ladies, and gentlemen can wear jackets and slacks. Shoes need rubber soles, but trainers are definitely taboo!

Whips (drivers) and passengers, but not grooms, wear aprons which are also correct for showing. If cold, a rug is more suitable and quite in order in the ring. The British Driving Society has the yellow carnation as a button hole and members of the Coaching Club wear a cornflower as the finishing touch.

John Parker is well known for his London to Norwich mail coach and his beautiful team of Hungarian horses and, as he rightly says, 'The trouble with carriage driving is that it looks so easy'. An enormously experienced driver, John Parker who has been driving for thirty-five years, runs the largest privately owned driving centre in Europe and offers useful advice.

❐ Don't think you can leave your horse in a stable or a field all week and he will go well on Sunday. You can't and he won't. He needs work.

❐ Do leave the collar and pad on him to warm up for ten minutes before you start work.

❐ Thinking only of the horses' well being (as always), John is critical of the new type of carriage for competitions which is designed to be narrow to get round obstacles on the marathon, but which does not provide quite enough width for comfort for two horses.

There are superstitions. When harnessing, the collar is always put on first and Sallie Walrond, LHHI, in her book '*Driving a Harness Horse*' says that, although not a superstitious person by nature, she would refuse to drive a horse harnessed any other way in case of accident. Sallie has been driving since the 1940s and is a respected authority on the subject of carriage driving. An international carriage driving judge as well as a council member, examiner and instructor for the British Driving Society, she was awarded the BDS Medal of Honour in 1991 for services to carriage driving.

Sallie's major complaint of lack of manners is towards riders or carriage drivers who fail to acknowledge the kindness of car drivers who slow down for horses. Her view is that the next time the irritated motorist meets a horse, he or she is less likely to take the trouble to slow down. It only takes a smile and a nod to say 'thank you'. Ignoring the polite drivers reflects badly on the rest of the horse community. Motorists can then accuse us of being 'stand-offish' and impolite.

Here are some more of Sallie's dislikes regarding the lack of courtesy:

❐ When she is proceeding with her turnout at an elegant park pace, only to be closely overtaken on the inside by a snorting, ground pounding, hard pulling animal whose driver has no regard for fellow competitors in an effort to impress the judge.

❐ When a pupil who books a day's carriage driving instruction, usually by telephone at fairly short notice, does not turn up. This makes her livid having spent hours cleaning the pony, harness and vehicle and she quite likely will have refused another engagement. She does not allow anyone who ever lets her down over a booking a second chance!

❐ People who write asking for help and advice about carriages, who invariably send photos which she feels duty bound to return and who do not enclose a stamp for the reply which usually takes her ages to type!

There are certainly plenty of do's and don'ts in the driving world.

Harness Racing

Harness racing is a sport which, although practised for over a hundred years, as an official sport, seems little known in Britain. It involves a horse and a very light weight carriage.

In 1879 the American Trotting Register considered it a fair standard that horses were able to trot or pace a mile in 2 minutes 30 seconds. Sometimes misnamed as trotting, the horses are, in fact, laterally gaited pacers.

It is an exciting sport for those taking part, perched on the seat of a sulky, and it is a thrilling sport to watch. There are now five established circuits in the UK with over thirty grass circuits. In this country, America and Australasia, pacing is the dominant gait, whereas European countries only allow trotting. Pacing, when the front and back legs on the same side move forward simultaneously, is about three seconds a mile faster than trotting with diagonal pairs.

Most harness racehorses in this country are American Standardbreds, known for their speed. The gaily dressed drivers on their delicate looking sulkies racing over a mile trying to break the two minute barrier are a fine spectacle. (If you decide to take part remember that all tracks except Musselburgh are on the left rein, anti-clockwise.)

Stella Havard is an experienced horsewoman who side-stepped into harness racing after a road accident put an end to her first career. Stella has run a racehorse livery yard and competed at national level across country and in the show jumping ring. Her informative book *'Harness Racing in the UK'* will tell you all you need to know about the sport.

Courtesy Check List
Harness Racing

✓   DO remember that if you are keen to enter a championship, you have to be a member of each appropriate association.

✓   DO join your local group to learn what is going on.

✓   DO get your lightweight horse shoes well in advance.

✓   DO remember that whip abuse is a punishable offence.

✓   DO be on time as lateness risks a fine.

✘   DON'T even think about buying a horse who throws himself on the ground when he decides he doesn't like the game.

✖   DON'T work out on the track without the appropriate number cloth or without wearing your colours, white trousers and skull cap, as this is an offence.

✖   DON'T wear trainers for driving; you could be banned. (In Florida you could also be banned for letting your wheels clash with another).

✖   DON'T put a headcollar on under the racing bridle as this will impose a fine.

✖   DON'T take your feet off the foot rests at any time as this will bring an instant fine. (If you do get fined for any reason you will be expected to pay before leaving the meeting).

✖   DON'T let your reins or number cloth be loose.

✖   DONT forget that once you are in competition, the only people you are allowed to talk to are the judges and stewards.

Mapping it Out –
Long Distance and
Endurance Riding

When the going gets rough, remember to keep calm.

Horace.

The stresses and strains of modern daily living seem to show themselves in mental ways, whereas the problems of the past were perhaps more physically related. If you had walked or cycled to work and then put in a hard day on a farm or in a factory, you would probably be happy to sit around in your rare moments of leisure.

Today, much more work is sedentary and therefore people are more likely to gain relaxation through expending their unused energy on physical pursuits. This could well account for the upsurge of interest in endurance riding, a sport where both horse and rider are physically and mentally tested.

On no account am I suggesting that the other equestrian disciplines do not also require this, but it is a very different kind of sport, needing a different kind of stamina.

A dictionary explanation of endurance, is a hardship, a strain or a privation, so that makes endurance riding a special kind of sport, with much staying power needed on the parts of both horse and rider. Strength and resilience are the key components which must be in place before any training begins.

One of the most interesting long distance rides in recent times could be that made by James Greenwood who spent ten years of his life riding different horses round the world. James gave up a promising banking career in the city to combine his favourite interests, riding and travel and to provide valuable research into the care of equines globally for the International League for the Protection of Horses.

Obsessed by 'Schiffley's Ride', an account of a solo trek from Buenos Aries to Washington DC in 1925, James resolved to take on a similar, but much more adventurous life style, reporting back to the ILPH on general conditions around the world, monitoring the practical measures needed to improve the environment for native horses.

From humble beginnings, present day endurance riding is now very much a competitive sport with countries competing against each other for various trophies. Britain won the first World Endurance Riding Championships in 1986 and the event is now held biennially.

Since the World Endurance Riding Championships held in the United Arab Emirates in 1998, a 100 mile race across the desert, more nations have been taking part, making it an increasing popular event on the world scene. No other equestrian discipline has fielded as many nations for a world championship and the organisers believe it will make a significant contribution to the international campaign to make endurance riding an Olympic discipline especially in view of the interest in the middle east.

In this sport, the importance of riding as part of a team is emphasised, as is the importance of goodwill towards other members of the team and the opposition. Dressing the same reinforces team solidarity and it is reputed that fewer butterflies in the stomach are experienced when a team get together at a strange venue all dressed the same!

Long distance riding can be a 10 to 20 mile pleasure ride to be completed within a certain time; after this, there are the competitive trail rides which have to be completed at a faster speed and where your horse must pass veterinary inspections to prove his fitness and make sure he is all right to carry on.

Endurance races over rough terrain, galloping over open moorland, fording rivers, climbing steep, rocky hillsides, are a true endurance test of horse and rider. Obviously you need to progress through a series of shorter rides to qualify both you and your horse in order to compete in endurance races.

To keep in tune with other equestrian disciplines, Endurance GB has changed the terminology in its rule books from bronze, silver and gold standard rides, to novice, intermediate and advanced classes.

The Horse

As with the other disciplines, choosing a horse for endurance riding needs great care. Any fit, sound horse or pony can be trained to compete in 20 and 30 mile rides, but if you want to compete more seriously, you will need an athletic horse, preferably one with some Arab or Thoroughbred blood, and often with some native pony in him.

Training needs to be started at least six weeks before the event, when you should do all the usual checks: worming, teeth, shoes, and so on. Shoes will wear out faster than usual when endurance riding so make a regular appointment with your farrier.

If your animal is hairy he will need clipping. You may get away with a low trace or belly clip. To get to the required level of fitness you will need to exercise your horse at least four or five times a week, with him having one or two days off. If he has two days off, try not to make them consecutive days and, if something unforeseen happens and a third crops up, put him in the field to loosen up rather than standing in the stable.

You will need to be able to judge your horse's natural speed and to get to grips with Ordnance Survey maps

You will need to be able to judge your horse's natural speed and get to grips with Ordnance Survey maps, especially if you are taking part in Le Trek, where you will need to orientate. Buy yourself a stethoscope and listen to your horse's heart; the vet will show you the correct way to do this, and then you will be able to compare your horse's resting pulse with that after exercise and at five minute intervals. The fitter your horse, the quicker his pulse and also his respiration will return to normal.

On the Ride

As in the other horse sports there is a rule book which must be read and absorbed. Many of the unwritten rules are the same as in other disciplines; for examples, your horse should be happy about passing other horses and being passed them. He must be able to have horses approaching from any direction without worrying and be confident alone or in a group. It goes without saying that he should be able to go first or last in company; easier said than done, that one!

If your horse is a novice, he should wear a green ribbon on his tail to let other people know this. If he is likely to kick he should wear a red one. As with any competitive event, do not try to make small talk with those preparing for it. Trying to relax the horse and yourself can be a daunting experience needing all the calm and quiet you can find. This is not the time for a chat.

It is a bonus if you can open and shut gates from your horse's back. If he is not good about this and there is the possibility that you may hold others up while he fusses about, you will be more popular if you dismount in order to save time in the long run.

If you need the farrier and there is a queue, wait your turn patiently. If your horse has cast a shoe, do not apportion blame. You need that farrier!

At check points, always wait your turn and thank the stewards, and, it should go without saying, obey them and the marshals at all times. Keep an eye out for others, especially young riders, to make sure they are safe. You would want someone to stop and help you if you were in trouble.

Passing a horse and rider must be done with care. Wait for a wide space and call to ask if it is all right to pass, then trot gently by until you are well in front. If you are riding with other less experienced riders, remember you were once in that situation. Do not overtake pretending your brakes have failed or because you are panicking and trying to make

On Saying Goodbye

'It lies in the lap of the gods'
Homer – The Iliad

No one likes discussing death and animal owners are often the worst section of the community in this respect. Some people shut off by refusing to talk about it and others become dramatic, proclaiming, 'I can't bear to even think of it!' regarding their horse, dog or cat.

It is a sad but inevitable fact of life, however, that none of us stays the course forever and while you devote your days to that of your horse during his lifetime, he is entitled to your whole-hearted concern for him at his time of death. You owe him that courtesy.

Perhaps the most awesome part of death is the realisation that no-one knows when that will be. It is, indeed, in the lap of the gods. The same cannot be said, however, of the way in which you handle the situation when it does come. Sudden death or accidental aside, this will be your decision and by knowing all the available options you will be better able to cope at such an emotional time.

Care in the Twighlight Years

I feel strongly that when you take on the responsibility of horse-owning, a great deal of thought should go into it before you buy. We have all seen the pet rescue programmes on television where people give up their horses to various societies for a number of reasons: lack of money, divorce, lack of grazing and so on, but I always think the worst scenario is when an ageing horse is sent to pastures new.

You cannot just abandon an old horse or pony in his twilight days. Putting him in a meadow and leaving him to get on with it, just because

You can not just abandon an old friend in his twilight days

you are not riding him any more, is not fair. It is cruel and negligent. He has been your friend and given of his best in his active days and now he needs, and deserves, tender loving care in retirement. An old horse needs a balanced diet to sustain him with plenty of good meadow hay. He also needs love and attention, as well as grooming, to maintain the human contact, and a warm comfortable bed for the night in a loose box or stable. (A cosy, warm bed gives as much benefit as an extra feed).

He needs his teeth attended to so that he can continue to eat successfully and he needs regular worming as before. All these things cost money, which is why I cannot reiterate strongly enough the need for careful thought before purchase.

I recently lost a pony aged 22 years. I had owned him since he was six months old. Twenty plus years is a long time to care continually for a pet. One of my ponies lived to be over 40 years old. All these factors have to be borne in mind when considering owning a horse of your own.

Your final choice

I remember once asking my farrier how most horses died. 'Their legs give out', he said succinctly 'and they have to be shot.' I was horrified at the time and persisted: 'But don't any ever die of natural causes?' 'Very rarely,' was his firm reply. Sadly, my years of horse owning have proved him right. Out of ten horses, only one died without human intervention.

You don't want to wait until the vet announces there is nothing more he or she can do for your horse before you decide on a method of disposal. You will have quite enough stress at that time without the burden of not knowing what to do afterwards. If you have made the decision previously, setting the wheels in motion gives you something else to think about.

If you want your vet to administer a lethal injection so that your horse goes to sleep and doesn't wake up again, you have to remember that the onus is usually upon you to dispose of the body.

An acquaintance of mine, knowing her horse was old and terminally ill, hired the services of a digger to prepare the grave before the horse died. This necessitates living with the practical imminence of saying goodbye, which could be a great emotional strain. The removal, however, would be swift and the burial over very quickly. Obviously, it has to be a very large excavation and this can only be done when you have sufficient land for it not to be a problem and there are no near neighbours to object. You would also need to remember that if you were to sell up and move, an explanation would be necessary to the new owners.

The other alternative is to have your horse shot. This is generally done with a humane killer, a captive bolt – not a rifle shot at long range with a telescopic sights. While this seems very cold blooded when viewed in print, it is the method I prefer. If your horse is suffering, then he needs to be put out of his misery as quickly as possible and this is the quickest method of all. I am not saying it is not distressing because it is and whichever method you choose, it will take a long time to recover from the loss.

With ten horses it was unrealistic to consider home burial so I have always used the services of the local hunt. A member of hunt staff, usually the kennel huntsman will bring a trailer and winch to lift the body. You are free to go away and leave them to get on with it. You need never worry about doing this as the person the hunt sends will be a 'horse person' sympathetic and used to handling them. I prefer to stay until the horse has gone.

Some veterinary practices will arrange to contact the hunt for you. Some hunts will arrange for cremation rather than food for hounds, but

I choose to think it is a form of recycling and giving back to nature. There are private crematoriums and prices differ from region to region. Where I live the hunt charges approximately £50 for removal of the body, depending on whether it is a pony or a horse.

Whichever method of euthanasia you choose you can only hope that everyone will be professional, sympathetic and efficient. You will also be reassured by the fact that you have mentally organised the event previously so that everything will go as smoothly as could be expected. By caring for your horse in death you will have completed the loving circle you began when he came in to your life.

Courtesy Check List
The final courtesy

✔ DO make some important decisions at the start of your relationship.

✔ DO make local inquiries to see what facilities are available.

✔ DO remember that the inevitable can happen at any time.

✔ DO be strong for the sake of your horse. He is sensitive to vibes and you will do him no favours by weeping and wailing in front of him. Be as natural and normal around him in his last few minutes as possible.

✔ DO remember that if your horse is old and your vet has been treating him for many years, the vet may need a strong cup of tea after he has administered the final treatment, as well as you.

✔ DO (if you don't want to be present when your horse's body is winched on) leave hunt staff with a bucket of sand, spade, broom and water. It is part of their job to clean up for you once the horse is loaded, but they wont be able to unless you have left the equipment ready.

Courtesy Check List
The final courtesy

✖ DON'T ignore the possibility, pretending it will never happen.

✖ DON'T leave the arrangements to another. You might regret it afterwards.

✖ DONT forget that keeping a horse who is actually suffering in order to avoid personal upset, represents disgraceful conduct.

My father, George Cadden, wrote the following poem for me
when he was 93 years old and I think it successfully epitomises the
bond forged between horse and rider

Fidelity

You little know, my trusted friend
Why I always talk of 'we'
For moments of the sweetest peace,
Complete tranquillity.

When friends despise, and some forsake
When cynics laugh with scorn,
With one accord I turn to you
To change my night to morn.

You never murmur nor complain
When treated with reserve.
Your perpetual thought appears to be –
My mistress I must serve.

Though people come and people go,
And empires snap in twain,
I pledge myself – my dearest steed
Till death shall snap the chain.

George Cadden

Other publications available from
COMPASS EQUESTRIAN

Title / *Author*	Price	Tick your order
A Young Person's Guide to Dressage *Jane Kidd*	£13.95	....
Focused Riding *Robert and Beverley Schinke*	£12.95	....
The BAHNM Dictionary of Holistic Horse Medicine and Management *Keith Allison*	£10.99	....
Astrology and Your Horse *Vicky and Beth Maloney*	£13.95	....
Riding for Gold - 50 Years of Horse Trials in Great Britain *Jane Pontifex*	£25.00	....

Compass Pony Guide Series {£2.99 each or £16.00 th set}

Book 1 - More Than Just A Pet	£2.99	....
Book 2 - Head First	£2.99	....
Book 3 - Bodywork	£2.99	....
Book 4 - Forelegs and Four Feet	£2.99	....
Book 5 - A Bit More Than A Mouth	£2.99	....
Book 6 - Top, Tail and Overcoat	£2.99	....
Book 7 - Filling Up The Tank	£2.99	....
Book 8 - Why Does He Do That?	£2.99	....

Compass Points for Riders Series

1. Snaffles *Carolyn Henderson*	£6.99	....
2. Training Aids *Carolyn Henderson*	£6.99	....
3. Plants, Potions and Oils for Horses *Chris Dyer*	£6.99	....
4. Drugs and Horses *Anne Holland*	£6.99	....
5 Gymnastics... *James C. Wofford*	£6.99	....
Words of a Horseman *Tina Sederholm*	£9.95	....
The Well Adjusted Dog *Dr. D. Kamen*	£9.99	....
The Well Adjusted Horse *Dr. D. Kamen*	£9.99	....
Points of a Pony / Poisonous Plants (Wallcharts)	£1.50	....

P&P   £2..50

Total =   £............

How to order: see overleaf...

TO ORDER   please send a cheque made payable to
Compass Equestrian Ltd

or VISA/MASTERCARD details

to

Cadborough Farm
Oldberrow
Henley-in-Arden
Warwickshire
B95 5NX

Tel: 01564 795136
email: compbook@globalnet.co.uk

Name: ....

Address: ....

....

....

Signature: ....

VISA no: ....

Expiry date: ....